BIBLE GUIDEBOOK

BIBLE
GUIDEBOOK

William N. McElrath
Illustrated by Don Fields

BROADMAN PRESS
Nashville, Tennessee

Dewey Decimal Number: 220
Library of Congress Catalog Card Number: 72-79174
Printed in the United States of America

CONTENTS

1
WHAT THE BIBLE IS

What is the Bible?

There are many ways to answer that question. Some people would immediately say, "God's Word." Some would point out that the Bible is the world's all-time best-selling book.

Preachers like to quote remarks from famous men, telling their opinions about the Bible. Creeds, or confessions of faith, contain statements defining the Bible.

Robinson Crusoe had not planned to include Bibles with his freight, but a friend loaded in three of them without his knowledge. He rafted them ashore onto his desert island along with other salvage from the wrecked ship, but didn't get around to beginning reading till almost nine months had gone by. Then he—like many another lonely exile or prisoner—found the Bible to be one of his dearest treasures:

"I never opened the Bible, or shut it, but my very soul within me blessed God for directing my friend in England, without any order of mine, to pack it up among my goods; and for assisting me afterwards to save it out of the wreck of the ship."

Yet, to many people today, the Bible is just "that black-covered book on the coffee table—the one nobody ever reads."

What is the Bible, actually?

A Holy Book

The Bible is a collection of books into one volume, considered holy or sacred by Christians of all groups.

In this collected volume there are two main sections: the Old Testament of thirty-nine books, and the New Testament of twenty-seven books. The Jewish religion joins the Christian faith in regarding the Old Testament as a holy book. Moslems also accept parts of the Bible as being sacred.

Judaism, Islam, and other religions also have other holy writings. But it is not correct to call these other sacred writings "Bibles." The word "bible" (without the capital letter) has come to be used to mean any kind of guidebook that a person depends on constantly. But really, there is only one Bible.

Members of various Christian churches have wide differences of opinion about how the Bible was written and how it should be interpreted and understood today. But all of them agree that the Bible is the holy book of their faith.

An Inspired Book

Christians often use such expressions as "the inspiration of the Scriptures" or "the inspired Word of God." What does it mean to say that the Bible is inspired?

"Inspired" literally means "breathed in." This word is also used about other writings than the Bible. It means that some great idea, some vision of beauty, was somehow "breathed in" to an author's mind so that he felt *inspired* to put it into words.

This is about all some people mean when they say that the

Bible is an inspired book. Certainly no book contains more great ideas or more visions of beauty.

For many Christians, however, this definition of inspiration is not enough when speaking of the Bible. They believe that in a unique way, God himself "breathed in" to the minds of the people who wrote the Bible.

Some Christians go so far as to say that the Bible authors had no real control over what they wrote—that they were almost like tape recorders, with God dictating into them. Other Christians believe that God inspired each Bible writer to use all of his own abilities, thoughts, impressions, and feelings.

Whatever it means to say that God inspired the writing of the Bible, it is plain that the Bible is both a divine and a human book. God's guidance of the process by which it came to be—however he did it—makes the Bible a divine book, the Word of God. The efforts of many writers—ordinary people except in their relationship with God—made the Bible a human book, a work of literature.

A Book of Books

Strange to say, the Bible itself does not call itself "the Bible." That exact word is nowhere found, in any of its sixty-six books.

How, then, did this holy Book come to be called "the Bible"? What does the word mean, and where did it come from?

It is interesting to learn that the word *paper* and the word *Bible* both come—not from the same word, but from the same plant. Papyrus reeds grow in marshes near the Nile river. Ages ago Egyptians discovered that the inner bark of these reeds, when dried and woven together, could be written upon. The word *paper,* of course, comes from *papyrus.* But the Greek word for that inner bark itself is *biblos.*

Biblos gradually came to mean "book," because that's what many ancient books were written on. *Biblion* meant "little book." Both of these words are used several times in the Bible.

Biblia, the plural word for *biblion,* appeared in the first Bible translation ever made: the Greek Old Testament. Authors even before the time of Christ began calling collections of sacred writings simply "little books." By five hundred years after Christ, that was the usual name for the combined Old and New Testaments.

In later centuries the word *Biblia* was no longer thought of as a plural word, "the Books." It began to be understood as a singular word, "the Book." Sixty-six books had come to be regarded as one Book of books.

From Greek and Latin, the word *Biblia* passed into modern European languages: in Spanish, *La Biblia;* in Dutch, *Het Bijbel;* in German, *Die Bibel;* in French, *La Bible;* in English, *The Bible.*

Two Testaments

What does it mean to say the Bible is composed of the Old Testament and the New Testament?

The word "testament," as used nowadays, usually refers to the document a person signs telling what he wants done with his property when he is dead: a "last will and testament." But the Bible mainly uses this word in an older meaning.

Actually, "Old Covenant" and "New Covenant" would be better titles for the two big divisions of the Bible. A covenant is an agreement, a solemn promise. The Old Testament tells how God made such an agreement with one man, Abraham, and with Abraham's descendants, the Hebrews (or Israelites or Jews). Everything in the Old Testament is either an introduction to this old covenant, or a record of how God kept his promise but God's people broke theirs.

A part of God's promise was that he would someday send a Savior, a great Leader for his people. The New Testament tells how God kept this most important part of his promise. Jesus Christ, Son of God and Savior of the world, lived on earth, died, and rose again to live forever more. God offers a new agreement or new covenant to anyone, of whatever race or place or time, who will commit his life to God through Jesus Christ. The New Testament also tells how Jesus' followers started the job (which still continues today) of sharing the good news about Jesus with people all over the world.

Thus the two Testaments tell one story: the story of God and his people. In the Old Testament God's people were Hebrews—especially those who were faithful to God's old covenant with Abraham's family. In the New Testament and ever since, God's people are Christians—not just those who like the sound of that name, but those who have truly surrendered their lives to become *Christ*-ians, or followers of Christ under the new covenant.

Sixty-six Books

The Bible is not only divided into two Testaments; it is also divided into sixty-six books. Jerome, who made the first translation of the entire Bible (into Latin), called it *"Bibliotheca Divina"*: "the Divine Library."

There is nothing special or sacred about that number sixty-six in the Bible library. In fact, the Jewish Old Testament, although it includes exactly the same material that we count as thirty-nine books in the English language, is counted as twenty-two or twenty-four books in the Hebrew language.

The sixty-six books of the Bible are greatly different one from another. Some are as long as books that would ordinarily be printed and bound in separate volumes. Some are less than one page long. Some are hard to read; some are easy. Some are prose; some are poetry. Some are meant to be taken literally; some use gorgeous picture-language.

Section 4 of this book is entitled "What the Bible Books Are About." In this section you will find all the books of the Bible arranged in alphabetical order. Each book has one or two pages of its own in this section, giving you a brief idea of what to expect when you turn to that book in your Bible.

The sixty-six Bible books can also be roughly divided according to groups or types. One way of dividing them that is often used is shown on page 11.

Remember that these divisions are not exact. For instance, there are many poems in Bible books not listed as "Poetry." And one "Poetry" book, Ecclesiastes, includes much prose. "Lamentations" is not the name of a prophet, as are the others listed under "Major Prophets." Also, Lamentations is shorter than some of the short books grouped as "Minor Prophets." There is history in books of Law, books of the prophets, and books of other types—not just in books marked "History."

Yet, these groupings are useful. They do give you a fair idea of what kind of material is most found, or is most important, in each section.

They are also helpful in remembering the arrangement of books as printed in your Bible. Notice similarities in names of groups and numbers of books:

OLD TESTAMENT

			Major	Minor
Law—5	History—12	Poetry—5	Prophets—5	Prophets—12

NEW TESTAMENT

		Paul's	General	
Biography—4	History—1	Letters—13	Letters—8	Prophecy—1

Many Versions and Translations

Not all Bibles look alike. They come in all sizes, thicknesses, and colors. Even when you open them, not all of them look alike. Some have verses divided as if each were a separate paragraph; some do not. Some print poetry in poetic lines; some print it the same as prose. The very words you read do not sound the same when you compare one kind of Bible with another.

Some people make this situation even more confusing. They insist that some certain kind of Bible is "the real Bible" or "the true Bible"—as if all others were false.

How did this confusion come to be? Are there really different Bibles? Are some of them good and others bad?

First of all, remember what the very beginning of this book said: There is only one Bible.

But if you had an *original* copy of that one Bible, could you read it? Try these two verses:

בראשית ברא אלהים את השמים ואת הארץ:

ΒΙΒΛΟΣΓΕΝΕΣΕΩΣΙΗΣΟΥΧΡΙΣΤ
ΟΥΥΙΟΥΔΑΥΕΙΔΥΙΟΥΑΒΡΑΑΜ

Are you having trouble reading these Bible verses? Perhaps it will help you to know that the top line is Genesis 1:1, the first verse in the Old Testament; and the bottom two lines are Matthew 1:1, the first verse in the New Testament. Genesis 1:1 is in Hebrew, the language in which most of the Old Testament was first written. Matthew 1:1 is in Greek, the language in which most of the New Testament was first written. (Very small parts of both Testaments were first written in Aramaic; it isn't easy to read, either.)

Here are the two verses using English letters:
HTRHTDNNVHHTDTRCDGGNNNGBHTN

THEBOOKOFTHEGENERATIONSOFJESUSCHRISTTHE SONOFDAVIDTHESONOFABRAHAM

Are you still having trouble with your Bible reading? Perhaps it will help you to know something else. Both Hebrew and Greek used to be written with no spaces between words, and all capital letters. Try separating Matthew 1:1 into words. Now can you read it?

Hebrew is a little harder. It was written at first with only consonants—no vowels. Let's separate words and put vowels where they belong in Genesis 1:1:

NEVAEH EHT DETAERC DOG GNINNIGEB EHT NI
HTRAE EHT DNA

Still no success? One more fact might help. English words are written from left to right across the page. But Hebrew words are written from right to left!

Perhaps all of this has helped you understand why there seem to be so many different Bibles—although there is really only one Bible. That one Bible was written in ancient languages which few people can understand today. The Bible has *had* to be translated into other languages, so everyone can read it.

Anytime something is taken over from one language into another, changes are bound to happen. And no two people are likely to translate something in exactly the same way. (Think for a moment: How many different ways can you say something that means "I like you"—even in the same language?)

Even if every word in the one original Bible could be precisely matched to one word in the English language, there still might need to be more than one translation of the Bible into English. Some versions should be simple, for easy reading. (A good example is *Today's English Version.*) Others should go deeper into moods and meanings of the Bible. (A good example is *The New English Bible.*)

Besides all of this, languages keep on changing. When the most popular of all Bible translations, the King James Version, was still new, "I prevented the dawning" meant "I got up before daybreak." But now when we read Psalm 119:147 in that translation from the year 1611, it makes us think somebody tried to stop the sun from rising!

So new translations are always being needed. And the same Bible translation may be printed on different papers, with different helps included, in different bindings, with different price tags. But remember: There is still only one Bible.

The Rest of This Book

Section 7 of this book tells more about "How the Bible Came to Us." It explains how, under God's patient guidance, the Bible grew—in many ways, from many sources. It also tells the exciting story of how the Bible has come down to us today. It lists some of the many good English translations of the Bible that are available.

The Bible grew over a period of about a thousand years. Its contents relate events that happened over a period much longer that that. Section 3 of this book is a timeline: "When the Bible Events Happened." You may want to refer to it now and then.

Perhaps you have more curiosity than knowledge about the Bible. Perhaps you've heard of the prodigal son, or the shepherd psalm, or the Ten Commandments, or the Beatitudes, or the love chapter . . . but you don't know exactly where to spot them in the Bible. Section 6 of this book is entitled "Where to Find Interesting Parts of the Bible." You may want to leaf through it now.

This BIBLE GUIDEBOOK is only one of many types of helps available to understanding the Bible. Some of these helps are found in the Bible itself: chapter and verse numbers, for instance. Section 5 of this book, "How to Use Bible Helps," may offer you some practical advice.

It is more important, though, to *read* the Bible than to read *about* the Bible. Section 2 of this book is called "How to Read the Bible." It suggests where to begin, ways to "find the handle" of a book as big and unusual as the Bible is.

Thus this book is just what it says it is: BIBLE GUIDEBOOK. It has little value by itself. But as a handy guide to reading and understanding the written Word of God, it may be just the book you've been needing for a long time.

2
HOW TO READ THE BIBLE

Probably more people have been scared off from reading the Bible by the mere *look* of it, than is the case with any other book.

The Bible is a big, long book; let us admit that to begin with. Most printings of it run well over a thousand pages. Seeing that many pages, often arranged in double columns, sometimes with small or dim print—no wonder many people never even try to read the Bible.

Those who do make the attempt sometimes fall by the way-side. They run into a chapter of family trees, like the first chapter of the first book in the New Testament, or a chapter of laws, like those in the second book of the Old Testament. Few people get a thrill out of reading such stuff as that . . . and so they stop.

Even an interesting part of the Bible can sometimes trip up those who start to read it. This especially happens if they are reading one of the older Bible translations. Some people can stand more "thee's," "thou's," "begat's," "hast's," and "nay's" than others.

If you have never read the Bible, or have never read it very much, you may especially need the suggestions given in the first part of this section. If you have already read quite a bit in the Bible, but would like for your Bible-reading to become more meaningful or more regular, you may especially need the suggestions given in the last part of this section.

Beginning to Read the Bible

Notice the arrangement of books and Testaments in your Bible. You will see that the New Testament is at the back end of the Bible. Yet, this is the end from which anyone ought to begin reading the Bible. If you have only a New Testament, not a complete Bible, don't worry about getting a Bible right away. There is plenty to read in the New Testament first.

However, there is one matter you should check before begin-

ning to read either the New Testament or the Old. See how old your Bible is. Not the age of the particular copy you have, or the date when it was printed: Try to find out (in the front pages of it) when that version was first published. Unless you can find a date at least within this present century, it would be a good idea to look for a new translation.

If you are already used to reading an older translation (such as the King James Version of 1611 or the Rheims-Douay Bible of 1582-1610), you may prefer to continue with it. But if you have never read much in the Bible, there is no reason whatever to slow yourself down with old-fashioned language and outdated meanings. Dozens of translations have been made in the twentieth century; several of them are listed in section 7 of this book. And even if you are familiar with an older version, you may be amazed at what you can get out of a newer one.

With a reasonably up-to-date translation in hand, then, open your Bible to the beginning of the New Testament. There you will find the very heart of the Bible: four books telling the life story of the Lord Jesus Christ.

The best place to begin reading the Bible would be to go straight through one or more of these four books: Matthew, Mark, Luke, John. Many people advise beginning with the book of John, because it gives the most explanations about who Jesus is and how we should relate our lives to his. Other Bible students suggest that the book of Mark is the best one to read first. It is the shortest, and tells the basic facts about Jesus in a fast-moving narrative.

How and when should you read? That's up to you. There are many advantages to reading at least a little from the Bible each day; see suggestions made in the last part of this section. However, there are also advantages to reading John or Mark the way you would probably read any other book: straight through, as soon as you can find time to finish it.

Reading one of the Gospels, or biographies of Jesus, may whet your appetite for the others. Certainly it will do you no harm to read all four of these books before you read anything else in the Bible.

Notice that the third Gospel, Luke, is really Volume 1 of a two-volume work. The second volume is Acts, which comes just after the four Gospels at the beginning of the New Testament. Reading these as two parts of the same book, you will get a rapid view of the entire historical period covered by the New Testament.

If you find that you want to go on from Acts to read the rest of the New Testament, feel free. Sooner or later you should certainly read all of it. However, there are parts of the Old Testament which you may actually find more interesting and more readable than those shorter New Testament books that come after Acts.

Where should you start reading the Old Testament?

Why not start at the beginning? You will find the first book in the Bible, Genesis, full of stories—more intriguing than most of those on today's paperback bookracks.

Sometime in your reading, you will want to get acquainted with the Psalms. There is no particular reason to read all of this book—at least, not at first. Instead, leaf through it. Stop anywhere your eye falls—on words of beauty, words of comfort, words that seem especially to speak to you. When you see such words, read the chapter in which you find them. Let this ancient devotional book begin to touch your heart, as it has reached the innermost souls of people for thousands of years.

One good plan for further Bible reading would be to read biographies. If you have read any one of the four Gospels, you have already read a biography of Jesus. If you have read Acts, you have already read biographies of Peter, Paul, and other early followers of Jesus. If you have read Genesis, you have already read biographies of Noah, Abraham, Isaac, Jacob and Esau, and Joseph and his brothers (not to mention fascinating stories about the women these men married).

Here is a list of several important Bible characters, with references to parts of the Bible that give their biographies. Not every reference about each character is given; but enough is given for you to read the most important parts of his or her life story.

ABRAHAM: Genesis 11-25.

JACOB: Genesis 25-35; 37; 42-49.

JOSEPH: Genesis 37; 39-50.

MOSES: Exodus 1-20; 24; 31-35; Numbers 10-14; 16-17; 20-21; 25; 27; Deuteronomy 31; 34.

JOSHUA: The entire book of Joshua.

GIDEON: Judges 6-8.

SAMSON: Judges 13-16.

RUTH: The entire book of Ruth.

SAMUEL: 1 Samuel 1-13; 15-16; 19; 25.

DAVID: 1 Samuel 16-31; the book of 2 Samuel; 1 Kings 1-2.

SOLOMON: 1 Kings 1-11.

ELIJAH: 1 Kings 17-19; 21; 2 Kings 1-2.

ELISHA: 1 Kings 19; 2 Kings 2-9; 13.

ISAIAH: Isaiah 6-8; 20; 36-39.

JEREMIAH: Jeremiah 1; 7; 11; 13; 16-22; 24-29; 32-44.

DANIEL: Daniel 1-2; 4-6.

ESTHER: The entire book of Esther.

NEHEMIAH: The entire book of Nehemiah.

JESUS: The entire books of Matthew, Mark, Luke, and John.

PETER: The entire book of Mark; Matthew 4; 16-18; Luke 5; 22; John 1; 13; 18-21; Acts 1-12; 15.

PAUL: Acts 7-9; 11-28; 2 Corinthians 11; Galatians 1-2.

For another approach to Bible reading, see "Bible Reading Suggestions," in section 6 of this book.

Continuing to Read the Bible

If you have already acted upon suggestions in the first part of this section, or if you have already read much of the Bible on your own, perhaps you still need help in making a habit of Bible reading. Or, you may need encouragement in finding Bible passages that you have thus far not run across in your reading.

Sooner or later you ought to read the entire Bible. Not that you will automatically get some special blessing from God because you have done so; not just so you can boast to other people . . . but unless you read it all, how can you really say you know what's in it? How can you be sure you haven't missed sections through which God wants especially to speak to you personally?

Here are several suggested ways to read all of the New Testament, or all of the Bible, within certain specified periods of time. One of them may be a plan that appeals to you:

1. Read five New Testament chapters every week. You will finish reading the New Testament in exactly one year.

2. Read one New Testament chapter every weekday, and four chapters on Sundays. You will finish reading the New Testament in six months.

3. Read one Bible chapter every day. You will finish reading the entire Bible in three years and three months.

4. Read three Bible chapters every weekday, and five chapters on Sundays. You will read the entire Bible in a little less than a year.

5. Read three Old Testament chapters and one New Testament chapter every day. When you finish the New Testament (after a little more than eight months), start it over again, one chapter a day. When you also finish the Old Testament (in about ten months), then start reading four New Testament chapters every day. In a little less than a year, you will have read all of the Old Testament once, and all of the New Testament twice.

6. Read one Old Testament chapter and one New Testament chapter every weekday. Read three Old Testament chapters and one New Testament chapter every Sunday. When you finish the New Testament, start over at its beginning. In a little less than two years, you will have read the entire Old Testament, and will have read the New Testament three times.

7. In January and February, read the Old Testament books from Genesis through Deuteronomy. In March and April, read the entire New Testament. In May and June, read the Old Testament books from Joshua through Esther. In July and August, read the Old Testament books from Job through Song of Solomon. In September and October, reread the entire New Testament. In November and December, read the Old Testament books from Isaiah through Malachi. In one year you will have read the entire Old Testament once and the entire New Testament twice.

8. For still another method of reading the Old Testament once and the New Testament twice during a year, follow this plan through fifty-two weeks:

1—Genesis 1-26
2—Genesis 27-50
3—Matthew
4—Mark
5—Exodus 1-21
6—Exodus 22-40
7—Luke
8—John
9—Leviticus
10—Acts
11—Numbers 1-18
12—Numbers 19-36
13—Romans; Galatians
14—1 and 2 Corinthians
15—Deuteronomy 1-17

16—Deuteronomy 18-34
17—Ephesians;
    Philippians;
    Colossians; 1 and 2
    Thessalonians; 1
    and 2 Timothy;
    Titus; Philemon
18—Hebrews; James; 1
    and 2 Peter
19—Joshua
20—1, 2, and 3 John;
    Jude; Revelation
21—Judges; Ruth
22—Job 1-31
23—Job 32-42;
    Ecclesiastes; Song
    of Solomon
24—1 Samuel
25—2 Samuel
26—Psalms 1-50

27—1 Kings
28—2 Kings
29—Psalms 51-100
30—1 Chronicles
31—2 Chronicles
32—Psalms 101-150
33—Ezra; Nehemiah;
    Esther
34—Proverbs
35—Matthew
36—Isaiah 1-35
37—Isaiah 36-66
38—Mark
39—Luke
40—Jeremiah 1-29
41—Jeremiah 30-52;
    Lamentations
42—John
43—Acts
44—Ezekiel 1-24

45—Ezekiel 25-48
46—Romans; Galatians
47—1 and 2 Corinthians
48—Daniel; Hosea;
    Joel; Amos
49—Ephesians;
    Philippians;
    Colossians; 1 and 2
    Thessalonians; 1
    and 2 Timothy;
    Titus; Philemon
50—Obadiah; Jonah;
    Micah; Nahum;
    Habakkuk;
    Zephaniah; Haggai;
    Zechariah; Malachi
51—Hebrews; James; 1
    and 2 Peter
52—1, 2, and 3 John;
    Jude; Revelation

Here are some do's and don't's that may help make your Bible reading more meaningful:

DO	DON'T
Do make Bible reading a habit—daily, if possible.	Don't read the Bible only when the notion strikes you.
Do read all of the Bible sooner or later—not just the easiest parts, or just your favorites.	Don't worry too much about parts you don't understand, or spend a long time on hard or boring passages.
Do make use of helps to Bible study—maps, concordances, dictionaries, commentaries.	Don't spend more time reading *about* the Bible than reading the Bible itself.
Do vary the way you read the Bible from time to time.	Don't always read the Bible in the same set chapter-a-day way.
Do read more often in the more important parts of the Bible: the Gospels and other books that are basic to knowing what the Bible is all about.	Don't read the Bible as if every word of it deserved the same amount of time and attention; don't forget that some sections are more important than others.
Do change the translation you are reading now and then.	Don't always read from the same version of the Bible.

Do use a Bible that has print large and clear enough to make reading pleasant.

Do try to keep in mind a general idea of Bible history, so that you can connect what you are reading with major events, and with what came before and after.

Do read aloud sometimes—to other people, or just for yourself.

Do vary occasionally the time of day when you read the Bible.

Do sometimes read an entire Bible book through at one sitting.

Do shift back and forth now and then between the Old Testament and the New Testament.

Do reread favorite parts of the Bible as often as you feel like it.

Do expect new understanding when you reread a familiar Bible passage.

Do try to become more and more familiar with the contents and arrangement of the Bible.

Do make an effort to memorize meaningful verses.

Do take advantage of opportunities to read and study the Bible with other people.

Do make use of schemes or lists for daily Bible reading—those in this book, those in church periodicals, those in devotional books.

Do read the Bible prayerfully and thoughtfully.

Do ask God to show you special messages for you personally as you read the Bible.

Do share what God teaches you through his written Word.

Don't think you have to or ought to squint at small, blurred type.

Don't make a habit of letting your Bible fall open at random; don't try to make each verse or passage stand alone, with no relationship to any other part of the Bible.

Don't always read silently—even when you are alone.

Don't read the Bible only at the same set hour, no matter what.

Don't always read just one chapter or a few verses at a time.

Don't feel you must plow straight through the Old Testament before starting again on the New.

Don't force yourself to read too often parts of the Bible that seem to say little to you personally.

Don't take the attitude: "Why should I look at these verses again? I've read them a dozen times."

Don't be content to have to fumble around with an index every time you want to find something.

Don't get hung up on memory work, especially if you dislike it.

Don't always go it alone in reading and studying the Bible.

Don't feel it is babyish or mechanical to follow a set plan for Bible reading; remember, you can depart from it if need be . . . but don't forget to keep on reading!

Don't read the Bible just like any other book.

Don't read the Bible purely out of literary or historical interest, or because you feel you ought to.

Don't keep to yourself all the blessings you will receive from Bible study.

Remember Robinson Crusoe's experience with the Bible, mentioned at the very beginning of this book?

When he finally got around to it after nine months on his desert island, Crusoe had a good plan in mind:

"JULY 4. In the morning I took the Bible: and beginning at the New Testament, I began seriously to read it; and imposed upon myself to read a while every morning and every night; not binding myself to the number of chapters, but as long as my thoughts should engage me. It was not long after I set seriously to this work, that I found my heart more deeply and sincerely affected. . . ."

3
WHEN THE BIBLE EVENTS HAPPENED

You might say that the Bible covers untold ages of time and eternity: It begins with the creation of the world and ends with a vision of the glories of heaven.

Or you might say that time is not really important in the Bible: It tells how man can have a right relationship with God—any man, anytime, relating to the God who is always there.

Yet it is important to know something about when Bible events happened. Many parts of the Bible come into focus only when we can match them with certain historical events.

The rest of this section is a timeline. As your eye moves across each two facing pages, you will see four columns: *"Years," "God's Chosen People," "Bible Books,"* and *"Other Nations."* Read these explanations first:

"Years"—Many dates from Bible times are still unknown. Before the time of Abraham, it is nearly impossible to peg them down at all. Beginning with Abraham and moving forward to the time of Christ and after, we can generally say that dates of Bible events become more and more exact. But don't be surprised if other books do not agree with this book on certain dates. Notice also that *"Years"* at first are marked at fifty-year gaps, while *"Years"* after Christ was born are marked at only ten-year gaps.

"God's Chosen People"—In Old Testament times, this means the Jews (or Hebrews or Israelites). In New Testament times, this means Christians of all nations; but to avoid confusion, information about the Jews is still included under this column, even in the New Testament part of the timeline.

"Bible Books"—These are listed on the timeline, not according to when they were written, but according to *when the events happened that they tell about* or have reference to.

"Other Nations"—This column includes information from outside Palestine—from Asia, Africa, Europe, and North and South America.

YEAR	**GOD'S CHOSEN PEOPLE**
2000 B.C.	

1950 B.C.

1900 B.C. Abraham moves from Ur in Chaldea (Mesopotamia) to Canaan
(Palestine).
Abraham visits Egypt and returns to Palestine.
Isaac is born to Abraham and Sarah.

1850 B.C.

The twins Jacob and Esau are born
to Isaac and Rebekah.

1800 B.C.

Jacob moves to Mesopotamia.

1750 B.C.

Jacob's family moves back to Palestine; the mother of Joseph,
Jacob's favorite son, dies on the way.
Joseph is carried to Egypt as a slave.

1700 B.C. Joseph becomes prime minister of Egypt.
Joseph moves his father's entire family (the Israelites)
to Egypt.

1650 B.C. Joseph and his brothers die; their descendants (the
Israelites) grow to become a large part of Egypt's population.

BIBLE BOOKS

Genesis
(continued)

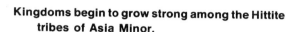

OTHER NATIONS

Egypt controls Palestine and Syria.
Donkey caravans travel between Ur and Egypt, passing through Canaan.

Kingdoms begin to grow strong among the Hittite tribes of Asia Minor.

A great sea-kingdom rules from its capital on the island of Crete.

Greeks begin to invade Crete.

Invaders from Palestine and Syria (Hyksos) conquer Egypt.

King Hammurabi of Babylon (Mesopotamia) passes his famous code of laws.

Exodus

YEAR	GOD'S CHOSEN PEOPLE

1600 B.C.

1550 B.C.

1500 B.C.

1450 B.C.   The Israelites (descendants of Abraham, Isaac, Jacob, and Joseph and his brothers) are made slaves and are forced to build cities for the Egyptians.

1400 B.C.

Moses is born to a slave family but is brought up in the Egyptian king's palace.

1350 B.C.

Moses commits murder and escapes to the Sinai desert.

1300 B.C.   Moses returns to Egypt; with God's help he leads the Israelites to freedom. God gives the Ten Commandments. The Israelites wander many years in the desert.

1250 B.C.   Joshua leads the Israelites to invade and to begin conquering Canaan (Palestine). Tribal chieftains (judges) rule the Israelites in Palestine; foreign tribes often invade the land.

BIBLE BOOKS

Exodus
(continued)

OTHER NATIONS

Pharaoh Ahmose I drives foreign invaders out of Egypt; an age of Egyptian power and progress begins.
Hittite tribes from Asia Minor destroy Babylon (Mesopotamia).

The Shang dynasty begins to rule China.
Aryan tribes settle in India, bringing with them the Hindu religion.

Pharaoh Thutmose III leads Egyptian war-chariots to victories in many lands.

The great sea-kingdom on the island of Crete falls to foreign invaders.

In Greece, the Mycenaean civilization reaches its peak.

Leviticus
Numbers

Deuteronomy
Joshua

Judges

Pharaoh Rameses II fights a great battle with Hittite tribes in Syria. Iron weapons begin to be used.

YEAR	GOD'S CHOSEN PEOPLE

1200 B.C.

1150 B.C.   The Philistines, a pirate tribe, land in Palestine and begin to attack the Israelites and other nations.

1100 B.C.   Deborah and Barak lead the Israelites to victory over the northern Canaanite tribes.

1050 B.C.   The Philistines crush the Israelites in battle.

1000 B.C.   Samuel crowns Saul as the first king of Israel.
David becomes a hero, then an outlaw.
David reigns as Israel's greatest king.

950 B.C.   Solomon becomes king and builds the Temple.

900 B.C.   After Solomon's death, his kingdom divides into the rival nations of Judah and Israel.

850 B.C.   Wicked King Ahab of Israel is challenged by the prophet Elijah.
Jehu kills the kings of both Israel and Judah on the same day; then he takes the throne of Israel.

BIBLE BOOKS

Judges
(continued)

Ruth

1 Samuel

2 Samuel   1 Chronicles

1 Kings   2 Chronicles

2 Kings

OTHER NATIONS

Greeks fight the famous Trojan War, finally
destroying Troy in Asia Minor.

Egypt begins to lose its power; priests
become its real rulers.

Maya civilization begins to develop in
Mexico.

Pharaoh Sheshonk (Shishak) leads
Egypt to invade Judah.

Assyria (Mesopotamia), growing in
power, fights a great battle in Syria.

The city of Carthage (in North Africa)
is founded.

YEAR	GOD'S CHOSEN PEOPLE

800 B.C.

King Jeroboam II extends Israel into nearby territories.

750 B.C.

Assyria defeats and destroys the kingdom of Israel.

700 B.C.   Assyria invades Judah, now ruled by good King Hezekiah.

650 B.C.

Good King Josiah leads Judah to return to God.
Josiah dies in battle. The prophet Jeremiah warns of God's
600 B.C.   coming judgment on his people.
Babylonia conquers Judah, takes many Israelites away as
     captives, and destroys Jerusalem.

550 B.C.

The Persian king encourages captive Jews (Israelites) to
     return to their ancestors' homeland.
Jews rebuild the Temple in Jerusalem.

500 B.C.

Ezra moves to Jerusalem and teaches God's laws.
450 B.C.   Nehemiah moves to Jerusalem
     and rebuilds the city wall.

32

BIBLE BOOKS

2 Kings	2 Chronicles
(continued)	
	Jonah
	Amos
	Hosea
Isaiah	
Micah	

OTHER NATIONS

Homer writes his famous epic poems.
Greeks hold the first Olympic games.

The city of Rome (Italy) is founded.
Assyria defeats the kingdom of Syria.

The first emperor of Japan begins to rule.

Jeremiah	Zephaniah
	Habakkuk
Daniel	Nahum
Ezekiel	
	Obadiah
	Lamentations

Assyria (Mesopotamia) falls to Babylonia.

Zoroaster teaches his beliefs in Persia.

	Ezra
Haggai	
Zechariah	
	Esther
Malachi	
	Nehemiah

Babylonia falls to Persia.
Buddha teaches his beliefs in India.
Confucius teaches his beliefs in China.

Cliff-dwellers settle in North America.
Greeks stop huge Persian invasions twice,
    at Marathon and Thermopylae.

Greeks enjoy a golden age of power
    and progress; famous dramas are
    written; gorgeous
    buildings and statues are created;
    great philosophies are taught by
    Socrates and others.

YEAR	GOD'S CHOSEN PEOPLE

400 B.C.   The Jews (Israelites) live in Palestine as one small part of the great Persian Empire.

350 B.C.

Greek language and culture influence the Jews, as a result of conquests by Alexander and his successors.
Greek kings of Egypt control Palestine.

300 B.C.

Scribes and scholars gather the books of the Old Testament and begin translating them into Greek.

250 B.C.

200 B.C.   Greek kings of Syria take over Palestine.

The Jews rebel, led by the Maccabee family; they win their independence by hard fighting.

150 B.C.

Jews destroy the capital city of Samaria; hatred grows between Jews and Samaritans.

100 B.C.

Rome conquers Palestine; the Herod family are set up as kings, under Roman control.

50 B.C.

King Herod the Great begins building a new Temple.
John the Baptist and Jesus are born.

BIBLE BOOKS

Joel

OTHER NATIONS

The great philosopher Plato teaches and writes in Greece.

Aristotle, Plato's pupil, tutors young Prince Alexander of Macedonia.

Philip, king of Macedonia, conquers Greece.
Philip's son Alexander the Great conquers the Persian Empire and other lands.
The Maya tribe in Mexico develops the most accurate calendar of ancient times.

Asoka, powerful king in India, spreads Buddhist beliefs.
Rome begins a long series of wars with Carthage, its most dangerous rival.
Chinese begin building their Great Wall.
Carthage, led by Hannibal, invades Italy.

Rome destroys Carthage and invades Greece.

Julius Caesar leads Rome to ever greater triumphs; he is murdered, but his great-nephew becomes the first Roman emperor.

Matthew   Luke

YEAR	GOD'S CHOSEN PEOPLE

10 B.C.

John the Baptist and Jesus are born.
King Herod the Great dies.

0

The boy Jesus visits Jerusalem.
Roman governors take over direct rule of Judea.

A.D. 10

A.D. 20

Jesus is baptized by John; he begins to teach, heal, and
    call people to follow him.

A.D. 30   Jesus is crucified by his enemies, but rises again.

Saul (Paul) becomes a follower of Jesus.

King Herod Agrippa rules Palestine under Roman

A.D. 40   control.

The apostle James is executed for his faith.
Paul begins his missionary journeys—to Cyprus, Asia Minor,

A.D. 50   Macedonia, and Greece.

Paul is arrested by his enemies in Jerusalem; after a long

A.D. 60   imprisonment and a dangerous voyage, he arrives in Rome.

Paul and Peter are executed in Rome.

BIBLE BOOKS	OTHER NATIONS
Matthew **Luke** (continued)	Under Augustus Caesar, Rome enjoys a golden age—in power, art, and literature.
	Parthians capture and rule what is now Pakistan.
	Augustus Caesar dies; Tiberius becomes emperor of Rome.
Mark **John**	
Acts **Galatians**	
	Rome conquers southern Britain.

1 Thessalonians
       2 Thessalonians
       1 Corinthians
 Romans   **2 Corinthians**
       Philippians
 James **1 Peter** **Ephesians**
    Philemon **Colossians**
 Titus **Hebrews** **1 Timothy**
    Jude   **2 Timothy**
   2 Peter
	Part of Rome burns; Emperor Nero blames and persecutes Christians.

YEAR	GOD'S CHOSEN PEOPLE

A.D. 70   Romans crush a Jewish revolt and destroy Jerusalem.

A.D. 80

A.D. 90

John, the last survivor of Jesus' twelve apostles, is exiled
to the Mediterranean island of Patmos.

A.D. 100   Jewish scholars make final decisions on which
books should be included in the Old Testament.

Ignatius, strong Christian leader in Syria, is taken to
Rome to be killed by wild animals in the arena.

A.D. 110

A.D. 120

A.D. 130

The Jews rebel again; Jerusalem is again destroyed and
replaced by a Roman settlement where no Jews may live.
The earliest known existing copy of part of a New Testament
book is written.

A.D. 140   The earliest known list of New Testament books is made.

In Africa, the Bible is partly translated into Old Latin.

BIBLE BOOKS

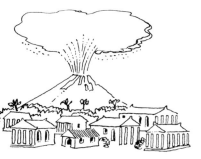

1 John   2 John   3 John

Revelation

OTHER NATIONS

Construction begins on the Colosseum in Rome.
Mount Vesuvius erupts and buries the Roman
cities of Pompeii and Herculaneum.

Rome conquers northern Britain.

The Roman emperor Domitian persecutes
Christians.

Korean kings first begin to rule in Korea.

Chinese invent the first real paper.

The Roman Empire reaches its largest size.

Northern barbarians invade India and set up
a new kingdom.

4

WHAT THE BIBLE BOOKS ARE ABOUT

ACTS

"Acts" is a shortened name for "The Acts of the Apostles." You will find it in the exact middle of the New Testament. It is the fifth New Testament book, very nearly the longest, and the only one grouped as History.

The books of Luke and Acts are Volume 1 and Volume 2 of a series. Both were written by Dr. Luke, a Greek physician who became the apostle Paul's close friend and missionary helper. Both of Luke's books were dedicated to someone named Theophilus; no one knows who he was.

"History" is not really the best term to describe Acts, although it does include much history from the thirty years just after Jesus' resurrection. Nor is "Acts of the Apostles" the best title, because it does not tell about most of Jesus' twelve apostles or disciples.

What Acts mainly does is to show how Christianity, starting out with just a few people in Jerusalem, spread into many important areas of the world. And because Christianity spread through *people* (as it always has), the book of Acts tells exciting stories about those people. Cornelius, the praying soldier . . . Philip, riding a chariot down a desert road while telling an African nobleman about Jesus . . . Stephen, who forgave the men that were stoning him to death . . . Dorcas, whose nimble fingers sewed new clothes for widows and orphans—these are some of the people you will meet in the pages of Acts. But the longest and most exciting adventures are those of only two men: Peter and Paul.

In the early days after Jesus ended his work on earth, Simon Peter became the main leader among Jesus' followers. He preached a sermon that helped three thousand people trust in Jesus. He dared Jesus' enemies to stop him from preaching. He healed sick people—even brought dead people back to life. He obeyed a vision from God that taught him that the good news about Jesus was for every man of every race.

Paul was a latecomer, compared to Peter and Jesus' other disciples. But he became the greatest missionary of his own time or any other time. At first he fought against the gospel and persecuted those who shared it. Then he met Jesus Christ one day on the road to Damascus. For the rest of his life, Paul could never stop telling the good news.

The book of Acts is one of the greatest collections of adventure stories ever written. This outline will guide your reading:
1. Jesus tells his followers to be his witnesses (chapter 1).
2. Jesus' followers witness in Jerusalem (2-7).
3. Jesus' followers witness in nearby places (8-12).
4. Jesus' followers witness in distant places (13-28).
   (1) Paul's first missionary journey (13-14).
   (2) An important meeting in Jerusalem (15:1-35).
   (3) Paul's second missionary journey (15:36 to 18:22).
   (4) Paul's third missionary journey (18:23 to 21:19).
   (5) Paul's journey from Jerusalem to Rome (21:20 to 28:16).

AMOS

Amos is located near the end of the Old Testament. It is placed third among twelve short books called the Minor Prophets.

Like most Bible books of prophecy, Amos takes its name from a prophet. His name happens to come first in the alphabet of all the better-known prophets. Maybe this can help you remember that he was also probably the first prophet whose prophecies were put into writing.

Amos lived in Tekoa—a rough, hilly place near Bethlehem. He was a farmer, taking care of sheep and fig-mulberry trees. When God called him as a prophet, he was not sent to people in his own land, the Southern Kingdom of Judah. Instead, Amos had to go to the rich, proud cities of Israel, the Northern Kingdom.

The Northern Kingdom had never seemed stronger than in the 770's B.C. King Jeroboam II's armies had conquered foreign enemies. In the capital city of Samaria, prosperous merchants had built gorgeous ivory palaces.

But God helped Amos see that all this wealth and pride were built on weak foundations. Israel's rulers despised and cheated the poor, needy people of the land. They pretended to worship God, while tricking and gouging their way to even greater power.

The second verse of chapter 1 of Amos says that the Lord God "roars" because of such evils. Amos' own voice must have sounded like the roar of a lion, when he dared stand up in the marketplace and tell the truth about the Northern Kingdom of Israel. King Jeroboam even sent his official priest to shut up the noisy troublemaker. But Amos kept on preaching.

The book of Amos does not tell much about Amos' own life. Verses 1:1 and 7:10-15 do give a little biographical information. But some of the most interesting verses are those that mirror conditions in the wicked Northern Kingdom. For instance, read Amos 2:6-8; 3:10; 4:1; 5:10-13; 6:4-6; 8:4-6.

Recent translations show clearly that most of the book of Amos was written in lively, colorful poetry. Since eight centuries before the birth of Christ, these stirring lines have warned people that God will not put up with wrongdoing forever.

1 CHRONICLES

First Chronicles is an Old Testament book placed about one third of the way from the front of your Bible. If you know what the word "Chronicles" means, it should not surprise you that 1 Chronicles is classified as a book of History.

In the Greek Old Testament, this book had a different name—a word meaning "Things That Were Left Out." That was not a bad title for Chronicles; read on to find out why.

Twelve books of the Bible come before 1 Chronicles. And 1 Chronicles is no less than a retelling of ten of those twelve books. Of course much of the story is retold in the shortest possible way; all you will find about Abraham, for instance, is that he had two sons named Isaac and Ishmael. But later history, especially the career of King David, is told in great detail. And, as that Greek book title suggests, 1 Chronicles adds some things you will not find in the books of 1 Samuel and 2 Samuel, which also give David's biography.

The writer of 1 Chronicles did not just add and take away as he pleased. Like all writers of Bible books, he was led by God's Spirit in his work. He had important purposes in mind.

First Chronicles was written long, long after King David's death. In fact, all the kings who had followed after him were dead and buried, too. Many people—even God's Chosen People, the Jews—had forgotten about those olden times. Of course, they could read stories of kings in other books. But the writer of 1 Chronicles tried to make sure people understood *why* the times of the kings had been a golden age in Israel's history.

The book of 1 Chronicles shows David as a great and good king because he was faithful to the Lord God. One main way David showed this faithfulness was in his attention to priests, sacrifices, and preparation for the building of the Temple.

Some people think Ezra wrote 1 Chronicles—the same Ezra in the Bible book by that name. But no one knows for sure who the inspired writer or writers were.

The first nine chapters of 1 Chronicles are almost entirely composed of family trees, going all the way back to Adam. Chapters 10 through 29, which retell David's story, make much more interesting reading.

2 CHRONICLES

Second Chronicles is a rather long book of the Old Testament. Because of the meaning of its name, you should not be surprised to find it near the end of the section called books of History. (In the Hebrew Bible, it was the very last book of the Old Testament, located where Malachi is in our Bibles of today.)

First and Second Chronicles used to be one long book. The first translation of the Old Testament ever made, into Greek, divided this long scroll into two parts. But both books were probably written at the same time by the same inspired person or persons.

Like 1 Chronicles, 2 Chronicles also is a retelling of history that we can read in other books as well. Second Chronicles covers the same years as 1 Kings and 2 Kings. However, there are important differences.

When 2 Chronicles was written, the Northern Kingdom of Israel had been gone so many hundreds of years that its records seemed like ancient history. This is why kings and prophets of the Northern Kingdom are hardly mentioned in 2 Chronicles. Almost all of its stories are about the Southern Kingdom of Judah, whose kings were all descendants of good King David.

Not that Judah was perfect—no, indeed! In fact, 2 Chronicles makes it plain that the Southern Kingdom fell at last because neither its kings nor its people were true to God. Yet, because of God's promises to David and his family, there was still hope for the future—if God's people would serve and worship God as they ought.

You might call 2 Chronicles a sermon based on history. Here is an outline of its main points:
1. Wise King Solomon succeeds good King David (chapters 1-9).
    (1) Solomon asks God to give him wisdom (1).
    (2) Solomon builds God's Temple (2-7).
    (3) Solomon rules long and wisely (8-9).
2. Solomon's descendants suceed him as kings (10-36).
    (1) The kingdom splits, as God's prophet predicts (10-11).
    (2) Kings rule in Judah—some true to God, some not (12-36).

COLOSSIANS

Colossians is a short book of the New Testament, located in the middle of Paul's Letters: Six other books in that group come before it, and six more after it. It was written by the apostle Paul to Christians in Colossae, a small city in Asia Minor (now Turkey).

Most of Paul's Letters were sent to old friends of his. In many cases, they had become Christians because of his influence. But Paul had probably never met the Colossian Christians. Perhaps this is why Colossians seems a little more formal and less warm than some of his other letters.

Paul was in prison when he wrote Colossians—probably in Rome. Some of his fellow-missionaries and other friends had told him about trouble in Colossae. Christians there were being bothered by false teachers.

"Of course it's necessary to trust in the Lord Jesus Christ," these teachers seemed to be saying. "But that's not enough. You must also go through certain ceremonies and obey certain rules."

The apostle Paul answered these misleading ideas by writing the book of Colossians. In it he made the clearest statement anywhere in the Bible that Jesus Christ is above all and in all and controls all things—that a life truly lived in faith and obedience to Christ needs nothing more whatsoever.

To make sure the Colossian Christians got the point, Paul used some favorite expressions and catch-phrases of those false teachers in Colossae. For instance, they had said that merely trusting in the Lord Jesus was not enough to bring complete "fulness" in life. Paul answered sharply that "all the fulness of God" was in Jesus Christ. (See Colossians 1:19.)

Paul's letter was carried back to Colossae by his friend Tychicus. At the same time Paul sent a shorter personal letter to Philemon, a member of the Colossian church. This note was carried by Onesimus, who had once been Philemon's slave.

Like many of Paul's Letters, Colossians has two main sections: one telling what to believe (chapters 1 and 2), the other telling how to act (chapters 3 and 4).

1 CORINTHIANS

First Corinthians is the second book in the group called Paul's Letters. It is also the second longest of all Paul's Letters.

The word "Corinthian" today makes people think mainly of two things: books in the Bible, and a certain graceful type of column first used in ancient Greek buildings. But when those buildings were still new, the word "Corinthian" had an entirely different meaning. It meant anything that was low, dirty, or immoral—anything that turned people's bodies into playthings for sexual games, drinking contests, and such.

That was the kind of city Corinth was when the apostle Paul first came there about A.D. 50. It was a big city—maybe 400,000 inhabitants. Trade from all over the Roman world flowed through Corinth.

Paul stayed there for more than a year and a half. He and his Christian friends Aquila and Priscilla won a good many other people to the Lord Jesus. But it might be expected that troubles would come up in a church located in a city like Corinth.

Some of those troubles were caused by wickedness and filthy living all around the new Corinthian Christians. Other troubles came from inexperienced leaders after Paul moved on: Some spread false teachings and questioned what Paul himself had taught. Others, through no fault of their own, became the centers of hero-worshiping clubs.

From Ephesus Paul wrote a letter to try to straighten out the mess in Corinth. This letter is mentioned in 1 Corinthians 5:9,11, but it seems that no copy of it was saved.

The church at Corinth answered Paul's letter. Three of its members came to Ephesus, bringing a long list of questions for Paul to answer. At about the same time Paul heard from other sources that arguments and bad behavior were about to wreck the Corinthian congregation.

Paul got busy writing again. The result was what we call 1 Corinthians (although it was really the second letter from Paul to the Corinthian Christians).

There are two main ways of dividing up the contents of 1 Corinthians. The simpler way is this: Chapters 1-6 have mainly to do with the bad news Paul had heard about the church at

Corinth; chapters 7-16 mainly have to do with questions church members themselves had asked him.

Another way of outlining it is in terms of relationships:
1. Relationships of leaders and groups inside the church (chapters 1-4).
2. Relationships between men and women (5-7).
3. Relationships between Christians and unbelievers (8-10).
4. Relationships of church members in worship (11-14).
5. Relationship between Christ's resurrection and Christians' resurrection (15).
6. Relationship between Paul personally and the Christians in Corinth (16).

The heart of 1 Corinthians, and the most famous part of it, is chapter 13. In just 13 verses Paul explained the key to all the problems in Corinth: *love.* If the Corinthians loved one another enough, they would not be quarreling about which teachings were correct or which leaders were best. They would not be falling into all kinds of sins, because true Christian love would leave no room in their lives for such things. No wonder "The Love Chapter" has been a favorite of many Christians through the ages!

2 CORINTHIANS

Second Corinthians is a book of the New Testament, located third in the group called Paul's Letters. The apostle Paul had already written three letters to the Christians at Corinth before he sent the one we call 2 Corinthians. His first and third letters seem to have been lost; what we have now in the Bible are actually his second and fourth letters. (Some Bible scholars think that the last four chapters of 2 Corinthians might be part of Paul's lost third letter that somehow got stuck onto the end of his fourth letter. This idea, however, has never been proved.)

Troubles in the new church at Corinth had not been solved by Paul's earlier letters, or even by a quick visit from Paul himself. And more and more there were false leaders who argued that Paul wasn't really an apostle of the Lord Jesus Christ.

Perhaps we ought to feel grateful toward those people who so greatly bothered Paul in the early days of Christianity. If it hadn't been for them, we might know a great deal less about Paul's life today.

Of course the book of Acts tells us much of Paul's story. But 2 Corinthians adds more of how Paul himself felt and acted than any other book. It even includes fascinating bits of biography that are not included anywhere else; for example, read 2 Corinthians 11:24-33. Second Corinthians 10:10 comes as close as any verse in the Bible to telling us what Paul looked like, and how he spoke.

But 2 Corinthians is not a selfish letter. In the midst of everything Paul felt forced to say about himself, he also included some of the clearest statements to be found anywhere, about how and why Christians ought to give freely to those in need.

This outline will help you read 2 Corinthians:
1. Paul answers those who were criticizing him and explains the greatness of being a minister of Christ (chapters 1-7).
2. Paul urges the Corinthian Christians to do their share in collecting a special offering for needy Christians in Jerusalem (8-9).
3. Paul defends himself as a true apostle of Jesus Christ (10-13).

DANIEL

Daniel is an Old Testament book, placed last in the section called Major Prophets. In the Hebrew Bible, however, Daniel was not called a book of prophecy. It was part of the last section of the Old Testament, which was called simply "the Writings."

Actually, neither "prophecy" nor "writing" best fits the book of Daniel. A better descriptive term is "apocalypse." This Greek word means "uncovering," or "opening up what is hidden," or "revealing." Another Bible book is also considered an apocalypse—the New Testament book Revelation.

Biblical apocalypse is different from other biblical prophecy in several ways: It tells about visions more. It uses more symbols, or words with hidden meanings. It predicts the future more. And it includes more prose than poetry.

The book of Daniel tells the story of a young Hebrew prince carried as a prisoner from Jerusalem to Babylon in the sixth century B.C. He and his friends Shadrach, Meshach, and Abednego remained true to the Lord God—even in a foreign land, when threatened by pagan kings. God protected and guided them in marvelous ways. Exciting stories about their experiences make up chapters 1-6, the first half of Daniel.

The second half of Daniel, chapters 7-12, is harder to understand. It truly fits the pattern of an apocalypse, for it tells about many strange visions. It speaks of times later than when Daniel lived. It stresses that the Lord God is more powerful than all the rulers of earth, and that those who trust in God will finally come out on the winning side.

Several of the best-known expressions in the Bible are found in the book of Daniel. Have you ever heard someone speak of "the handwriting on the wall"? That story is in chapter 5. Nearly everyone knows about "Daniel in the lions' den"; see chapter 6. A famous spiritual sings of "the Hebrew children"; chapter 3 tells about them.

No one knows when the book of Daniel was written—whether during the later part of Daniel's life, or long afterward. But disagreements over the date of writing, and over the meaning of Daniel's visions, do not make the book any less true, less interesting, or less inspired by God.

DEUTERONOMY

"Deuteronomy" is a strange book title, that came into being in a strange way. Yet, the title fits this rather long and important Old Testament book—the fifth and last book in the Law section.

When the first Bible translation was made long ago, someone misunderstood the Hebrew words in Deuteronomy 17:18 meaning "a copy of this law." Instead, he wrote a Greek word that meant "this second law." From that word comes the present book title.

Actually, Deuteronomy *is* like a second telling or repetition of the law. Long after God had first given the Ten Commandments at Mount Sinai, the Israelite people had at last come to the borders of the Promised Land. Soon they would march in and conquer it. Moses wanted to make sure they would stay true to God.

Most of the book of Deuteronomy is in the form of three long speeches or sermons delivered by Moses. He reminded the Israelites of all that God had done for them in the past. He urged them to remember their promises to God in the future.

Besides reviewing the Ten Commandments, Moses also stated a brief summary of man's duty to the true God: Not only must we trust, obey, and reverence him; we must also love him. This summary of the book is found in Deuteronomy 6:4-5. It is so important that every child in a faithful Jewish family, through all the centuries that followed, has memorized it. Jesus himself quoted it one day when asked to state the greatest of all laws (see Matthew 22:37). Jesus also quoted from this book when he was resisting temptations to do wrong; see Matthew 4:4,7,10.

Deuteronomy is sometimes called "the fifth book of Moses." But Moses could hardly have written all of it, because the last chapter tells about his own death and burial. Some people believe that certain unknown but God-inspired writers gathered together materials long after Moses' time to make up what we now know as Deuteronomy. Other people, however, believe that nearly all of the book was written by Moses himself.

Probably a copy of Deuteronomy was the lost book of the law that was found when the Temple was repaired during the days of King Josiah; it sparked a great revival and a return to God. (Read 2 Kings 22-23.)

ECCLESIASTES

Ecclesiastes is a strange name for a strange book. This rather short Old Testament book is placed just past the middle of the Bible, in the section called Poetry. Yet, it has more prose than poetry in it. It is often called a book of "wisdom." Yet, it is entirely different from Job and Proverbs, two other books of "wisdon."

"Ecclesiastes" comes from a Greek word (and before that, from a Hebrew word) meaning "assembly-man." This could mean someone who assembles people in a group or assembles wise sayings in a book. Or, it could mean someone who teaches or preaches before an assembly of people.

Who was this "assembly-man"? Verses 1 and 12 of chapter 1 of Ecclesiastes have caused many people to think that he was King Solomon. Yet, the book itself does not plainly say so. In fact, in Ecclesiastes 1:12 this strange "assembly-man" seems to speak of a time when he *used to be* king in Jerusalem. Solomon could hardly have written that, for he was king till he died.

Probably the "assembly-man" was a Jewish scholar and teacher who lived long after the time of King Solomon. He had looked and listened a long time to what went on around him. He had thought and prayed about what it all meant. The result of all this he put down in the book of Ecclesiastes.

Many people think of Ecclesiastes as the most gloomy book in the Bible. Certainly the "assembly-man" did not look on the bright side of things. He knew there was much in human life that hurts—much that is hard to understand, if we believe in a loving and powerful God.

Throughout his book the "assembly-man" mentions wealth, pleasure, knowledge, and other ways people try to find happiness in life. He decides that all of these are false—just like mere puffs of air. This is the real meaning of his famous and repeated expression, "Vanity of vanities! All is vanity" (Ecclesiastes 1:2; 12:8).

How, then, does this strange "assembly-man" tell us to make the best of things in a sad, confused world? "Work hard at whatever job you have to do." (See Ecclesiastes 9:10.) "Remember God your Creator while you are still young" (12:1). "Respect and obey God, who knows and judges all things" (12:13-14).

EPHESIANS

Ephesians is a book of the New Testament, placed fifth in the section called Paul's Letters. Clearly enough it is a letter *from* the apostle Paul; but there is a question about whether it really is a letter *to* the Ephesian Christians. Two of the earliest copies of this book that still exist do not have the word "Ephesus" in the first verse of the first chapter.

Perhaps what we call "Ephesians" was really a round-robin letter or circular which Paul sent to churches in several different places. Certainly its contents need to be read and studied by members of any Christian church—anywhere, anytime.

The most important idea in the book of Ephesians is *unity* or *oneness.* Christ, through his saving life and death and resurrection, has given all believers oneness with God. Because of this, all believers have oneness among themselves. Race, nation, background, culture—nothing should divide Christians one from another, because all are one through the Lord Jesus Christ.

These are big ideas. In expressing them, Paul used big words and long sentences. Twice he interrupted himself to pray—some of the most noble, moving prayers in all the Bible. (See Ephesians 1:15-23 and 3:14-21.) A modern-language translation or simplified version will probably be of special help to you in reading this great book.

Notice that the two main sections in Ephesians are much like the two main sections in several of Paul's other letters—the first section telling what to believe, the last section telling how to act:

1. What a Christian is toward God (chapters 1-3):
   (1) God's child (1:1 to 2:10).
   (2) A member of Christ's body, the church (2:10 to 3:21).
2. What a Christian is toward men (4-6):
   (1) A person who does what is right (4:1 to 6:9).
   (2) A soldier who fights what is wrong (6:10-24).

You will especially enjoy reading those last few verses. When he wrote Ephesians, Paul was guarded by Roman soldiers. He noticed every detail of their armor and weapons; then he used these in striking picture-language about Christian soldiers.

ESTHER

Esther is a short Old Testament book, placed last in the section called History. The Hebrew Bible placed it instead in the last group of Old Testament books, called simply "the Writings."

The main character of Esther is a Jewish girl who lived during times when Jews were in exile, ruled by Persians. She and her cousin and foster-father, Mordecai, managed to outwit a wicked plot and thus saved their whole race from being wiped out. One of many dramatic moments in this lively story came when Esther took her life in her hands by going into the Persian courtroom without permission. The king held out his golden scepter, and Esther was able to win him over to her side.

Esther is the only book in the Bible that does not mention the name of God. Besides that, it tells of taking revenge on enemies and of punishing innocent people along with guilty ones.

We must remember that Esther is in the Old Testament, not the New. It tells us nothing of Christ's love and forgiveness. But it does tell us that God is mighty, and will help those who trust in him.

EXODUS

Exodus is the second book of the Bible, one of the longest, and also one of the most important. It is grouped with the first Old Testament section, Law; but its contents cover much more.

The word "Exodus" has the same root as the word "exit," and the meanings of the two words are similar. Both have to do with "going out," which is just what the Israelite people did in the most famous happening recorded in the book of Exodus.

Exodus begins the biography of the most important character of the Old Testament: Moses. We meet him in chapter 2, as a baby hidden in a basket among the river reeds to escape a cruel king's sentence of death. The rest of Exodus, and the three books just after Exodus, all tell Moses' story or at least have something to do with him.

Yet, Moses' life story—exciting as it is—does not make Exodus such an important book. Its main character is really God himself. Its main event came when he saved his Chosen People by helping them escape from slavery in Egypt. He forced the Egyptians to free them, opened a way for them through the sea, and drowned the army chasing them.

Ever after that, the Israelites looked back on this tremendous experience as the real beginning of their nation. Before this, the Lord God had had a special agreement with Abraham and his son and son's son. Now God showed his mighty power to thousands of Abraham's descendants. And he extended his covenant, his special promise, to all of these people, the Israelites. At Mount Sinai they pledged themselves to serve the Lord God forever. God had the right to order them to keep his laws.

In a way, the book of Exodus is just as important for the Old Testament as the four Gospels are for the New Testament. Each of them tells what the rest of the Testament is talking about. Exodus tells of God's great saving acts in Egypt and at the Red Sea. The four Gospels tell of God's great saving acts in the Lord Jesus Christ. The rest of the Old Testament mentions the escape from Egypt again and again, along with a special ceremony to commemorate it: Passover.

This outline will help you find some of the many exciting stories in the book of Exodus:
1. The Israelites in Egypt (chapters 1-12).
   (1) Hard times burden the Israelites (1).
   (2) Moses is born, protected, and prepared for leadership (2).
   (3) God calls Moses from a burning bush (3-4).
   (4) God leads Moses to challenge Pharaoh, king of Egypt (5-11).
   (5) The first Passover feast is celebrated (12).
2. The Israelites in the desert (13-18).
   (1) They escape from Egypt and through the sea (13-14).
   (2) They sing in triumph and thanksgiving (15).
   (3) They journey toward Mount Sinai (16-18).
3. The Israelites at Mount Sinai (19-40).
   (1) They promise to keep God's covenant (19).
   (2) Through Moses God gives the Ten Commandments (20).
   (3) God gives them other laws (21-31).
   (4) They forget God and worship a golden calf (32).
   (5) God gives them his laws again (33-34).
   (6) They build God's holy tent or tabernacle (35-40).

EZEKIEL

Ezekiel is one of the longer Old Testament books. It is placed in the section called Major Prophets. Like the book just after it, Daniel, Ezekiel may also be described as an *"apocalypse."*

The prophet Ezekiel was taken into captivity from Judah, his homeland, about ten years before that country was destroyed by the Babylonians. In Babylon he warned his fellow exiles that their capital and holy city, Jerusalem, would be wrecked as punishment for their sins. When this sad prophecy came true in 587 B.C., Ezekiel then changed his theme and began to preach a message of comfort. He promised in the Lord's name that God's people would someday be allowed to return to the place their ancestors had been forced to leave.

Despite the great length of Ezekiel's book, it tells us very little about the prophet himself. In fact his name is mentioned only twice in all its forty-eight chapters. We know that he was married and that his beloved wife died in Babylon. We know that he acted out some of his inspired prophecies. But we mainly know Ezekiel only through what he wrote.

His book is one of the hardest of all Bible books to read, partly because so much of it is in the form of an apocalypse. Among apocalyptic features to be found in Ezekiel are these: much talk about seeing marvelous visions; many symbols, or words with hidden meanings; frequent predictions of future events; and more use of prose than poetry.

People have puzzled and disagreed for centuries about the meanings of visions and strange sayings in Ezekiel. Some Jewish teachers ruled that nobody under the age of thirty should even try to read Ezekiel, let alone explain it!

Yet, Ezekiel does have its values. Chapters 18 and 33 state clearly that (1) each person must make his own decision about serving and obeying the Lord God—no one else can do it for him; but that (2) a person who has rightly made this all-important decision is then responsible for telling others about the true God.

And, of course, some lively old spirituals are based on Ezekiel's peculiar visions about wheels (chapter 1) and about dry bones (chapter 37).

EZRA

Ezra is an Old Testament book of History. Although it is located a little before the middle of the Old Testament, a better place for it might be near the very end. It narrates the history of one of the latest periods told about in the Old Testament. Its ten chapters are almost the only description the Bible gives of what happened in and near Jerusalem from 539 to 458 B.C.

Like many Bible books, Ezra is named after one of its main characters. He may also have been author of the book, but there is no way to be sure about this.

In 539 B.C. King Cyrus of Persia conquered the Babylonian Empire. With it he inherited a large number of Jews and other captive peoples who had been forced to leave their native countries. Cyrus decided to change this policy. He encouraged displaced persons to return to their homelands.

The first group of Jewish exiles to head back toward Jerusalem was led by a member of the former royal family. The first chapters of Ezra tell how this group of almost fifty thousand refugees began to rebuild God's Temple (chapters 1-3). But enemies soon put a stop to their work (chapter 4).

Ezra's narrative then skips almost twenty years, to 520 B.C. At that time the prophets Haggai and Zechariah (the same ones whose messages are found in Bible books by those names) encouraged the Jews to get to work on the Temple again. The Lord's new house of worship was finished by 515 B.C. (chapters 5-6).

Again the book of Ezra passes over a long period of time. Not until 458 B.C. does Ezra himself come into the story. He was a scribe, who studied and taught God's laws. By order of the Persian king, he led a small group back to Jerusalem. There he found that many laws had been broken or forgotten. He got busy straightening out such matters (chapters 7-10).

The book of Ezra shows why the teaching and obeying of God's laws became so important to Jews in the later years of Old Testament history. They had no king of their own; their country had been conquered, their people scattered. God's Word given through Moses seemed the only thing left to pull them together as a nation.

GALATIANS

Galatians is a short book of the New Testament. It is placed fourth in order among Paul's Letters.

Galatia was a part of Asia Minor (now Turkey) which had been settled by Gauls—the same tribes that also settled what is now France. On his first missionary journey Paul started churches in several Galatian cities. He visited them again on his second and third journeys.

But Paul was not the only teacher who visited Galatia. A group of Jewish Christians also came there. "Jesus was a Jew," they pointed out. "His followers must all be Jews, too. Only by becoming a Jew can you become a real Christian." Many Galatian Christians believed these teachers. They began to try to obey all the old Jewish laws.

Paul was furious when he heard about this. His feelings were not helped any when he heard that those Jewish teachers had also been saying that Paul himself was not a real apostle, because he was not one of Jesus' original twelve disciples.

In reply Paul wrote the blistering letter we call Galatians. Read it in a modern translation to see just how mad Paul was and how sharply he attacked all those false ideas. "You are either fools, or else someone has cast a spell over you," he charged. "In my preaching you could see the Lord Jesus dying for you on the cross; what more do you need for salvation than to believe in him?" (See Galatians 2:16; 3:1.)

Perhaps we should be grateful for those unnamed Jewish teachers who gave the apostle Paul such a hard time. If it had not been for them, we would know much less of Paul's thrilling story. In proving that he was a genuine missionary for Christ, Paul told several fascinating details from his own life.

This outline will help you read the four-page bombshell Paul exploded when his letter arrived in the churches of Galatia:
1. Paul defends himself as a true apostle, and his teaching as the true way of becoming a Christian (chapters 1-2).
2. Paul explains that the only thing necessary for salvation is Christ's death for our sins; nothing else need be added (3-4).
3. Paul explains how Christians, who are free from the old Jewish laws, ought to live and serve their Lord (5-6).

GENESIS

Genesis is the first book of the Bible, one of the longest, and one of the most important. It is placed in the Old Testament section called Law, although that name hardly seems to fit it.

Actually, Genesis is best described by its own title. The Greek word "genesis" means beginning or origin. In the Hebrew Bible this book was called by its first word, which meant "In the beginning." And that is exactly what Genesis is all about.

Not only does Genesis tell—in beautiful, majestic phrases— about the beginnings of heaven and earth. It also tells about the beginnings of the human race, of sin, of God's dealings with man. It tells of the beginnings of a tribe that God called into special partnership with himself: Abraham and his descendants.

The book of Genesis has probably caused more trouble and disagreement among Christians than any other book in the Bible. Most of the difficulty has come about because of what Genesis does *not* tell, rather than what it does tell.

Genesis does *not* tell exactly when or how the universe was created. It does tell who created it: Almighty God. Genesis is *not* a scientific book; it is a religious book. Keep that in mind as you read it.

Another fact Genesis does *not* tell is, who wrote the book. Many people think Moses did. This idea has been held for thousands of years, and it may be right. But the book of Genesis itself does not say so, and many other people think several authors were inspired by God to do the writing.

None of these arguments should bother you when you read Genesis. Surely, you *will* read it: There is no more exciting storybook anywhere, inside or outside the Bible.

Probably you have already read many of the stories in Genesis. But maybe you haven't realized that all of those stories come from the same great book of the Bible. Adam and Eve, Cain and Abel, Noah, Abraham, Isaac, Jacob and Esau, Leah and Rachel, Joseph and his brothers—all of these are narrated in Genesis.

But the most important story in Genesis is the story of God himself—God who is all-powerful, all-knowing, all-loving. God controlled all the processes that caused the universe to come to

be. He showed his love to mankind by giving them the good earth to live upon. When mankind deliberately chose to do their own thing instead of obeying God, he punished them for their sin. But he still loved them. And through the family of one faithful believer, Abraham, God began to work a great plan to bring all mankind back into loving fellowship with himself.

This outline will help you read Genesis. It will probably take you several hours; but it will be worth it.

1. The beginnings of mankind (chapters 1-11).
    (1) The creation (1-2).
    (2) Man's fall into sin (3-4).
    (3) Early family trees (5).
    (4) Noah and the flood (6-9).
    (5) More family trees (10-11).
2. The beginnings of God's Chosen People (12-50).
    (1) The story of Abraham (12:1 to 25:18).
    (2) The story of Isaac (25:19 to 26:35).
    (3) The story of Jacob (27-36; 38).
    (4) The story of Joseph (37; 39-50).

HABAKKUK

Habakkuk is an unusual name for an unusual book. It is one of the Old Testament's shortest books, located near the end of the section called Minor Prophets.

No one knows anything for sure about Habakkuk except that he was a prophet. No one else in all the Bible was called by that peculiar-looking and peculiar-sounding name. No one is even sure what, exactly, the name means in the Hebrew language.

Even more unusual is the approach the prophet takes in his brief book. Most prophetic books speak for God to mankind. Habakkuk does that, too—but first it speaks for mankind to God. The prophet asks hard questions, and waits expectantly for God to answer them.

Habakkuk's first question was one that a thoughtful person might ask anytime, anywhere: Why do bad people seem to get along so well in the world? God's answer was that the Chaldeans (or Babylonians) would punish wicked Judah, the prophet's own country, by conquering it in battle. This prophecy came true, probably only a few years after it was first announced.

But Habakkuk wasn't satisfied. His second question was even harder: Why was God planning to use, as his tool to punish wicked Judah, a nation that was even *more* wicked? God answered that wicked Chaldea would also be punished.

But an even more basic answer to Habakkuk's question came in a famous phrase that has been quoted many times (including by the apostle Paul in the New Testament book of Romans): "The just shall live by his faith" (Habakkuk 2:4). In other words, a just or righteous man has faith in God; he believes that God will somehow work things out, even in a world where wrong often seems stronger than right. Through this faith in God, a just man can live in peace.

The third of Habakkuk's three chapters is a psalm—as beautiful as any you will find in the book of Psalms. Its last few verses, Habakkuk 3:17-19, sing in gorgeous poetic lines a firm confidence in God's goodness and power.

HAGGAI

Haggai is the second shortest book of the Old Testament. It is near the end of the final section called Minor Prophets.

Little is known about Haggai, except that he was living in Jerusalem in the year 520 B.C. Perhaps Haggai was at that time an old, old man; some verses in his book make us think he might have been able to remember the former Temple in Jerusalem, which had been burned in 587 B.C.

The first Jewish refugees who came back to their conquered homeland had begun to rebuild the Temple. This work had stopped, however, when enemies made trouble. For about sixteen years nothing had been done.

People kept saying they had no time or money to build God's house; yet they were busily building houses for themselves.

From September to December of the year 520 B.C., Haggai delivered four sermons to the people of Jerusalem. He pointed out how mixed up they were as to the important job. He urged them to get on with the Temple-building project. He predicted good things to come, if they would put first things first.

HEBREWS

Hebrews is the first New Testament book in the group called General Letters. It is the longest book in that section, and also longer than any of Paul's Letters except two.

Yet, it does not begin like a letter. Letters in Bible times usually began with the name of the writer. Hebrews does not, and Christians have tried and failed for many centuries to figure out who wrote it.

The title "To the Hebrews" is also not found in the book itself. However, it is plain that the people who were supposed to read and hear its contents were Hebrews who had become Christians. No one knows whether they were a small group in one place or Jewish believers in many places.

It is clear that these Jewish Christians were having a hard time. They were being persecuted—by their fellow Jews who did not believe Jesus was God's promised Messiah, or by Roman officials, or by both. Some of them were being tempted to slip back into their old Jewish religion to avoid persecution.

The writer of Hebrews, whoever he was, knew the Old Testament and the Jewish faith. Clearly, carefully, writing perhaps the most beautiful Greek found anywhere in the New Testament, he explained that Jesus Christ was far greater than anything in the ancient Jewish religion—Temple, sacrifices, priests, even Moses or Joshua.

Jesus himself, says Hebrews, is like a great high priest. There is no need for any other priest to keep on offering sacrifices, because Jesus the Son of God has offered the sacrifice of his own life and death. This gives salvation to all who trust in him.

Hebrews is one of the hardest books of the Bible to read with understanding. A recent translation will help. So will some background reading in the first five books of the Bible. But even if you read nothing else in Hebrews, don't miss these:

1. Jesus, both a heavenly high priest and a human being who understands our problems (4:14-16).
2. The hall of fame for heroes of faith (11:1-40).
3. Running the race of life as a follower of Christ (12:1-2).
4. Practical advice for Christians (13:1-19).
5. A great benediction (13:20-21).

HOSEA

Hosea is the first book in the Old Testament section called Minor Prophets. It is one of the longest of those twelve books, and one of the earliest in the history of God's Chosen People.

Elijah, Elisha, and Micaiah were great prophets who lived in Israel, the Northern Kingdom. None of them, however, left a written record of his prophecies. Amos prophesied in Israel, but he was actually a foreigner from Judah, the Southern Kingdom. Hosea is the only prophet of the Northern Kingdom whose words were written down in book form.

The name "Hosea" is really the same in Hebrew as the name "Joshua"; both are Hebrew forms of the same name as "Jesus" in the Greek language. This can help you remember that Hosea's prophetic message was perhaps more like the life and teachings of Jesus than the message of any other prophet.

Hosea emphasized God's great love. Over and over he used a Hebrew word to describe it: a word sometimes translated "mercy," sometimes "loving-kindness," sometimes "steadfast love." "The Lord God loves his people," Hosea preached. "Even when they sin and turn away from him, still he loves them. He calls them to come back into right relationship with him."

This great message in Hosea's sermons grew out of a sad fact in Hosea's life. The story is not completely clear in detail, but it appears that Hosea's wife Gomer was untrue to him. She gave herself to other lovers, and finally even became a prostitute—a woman who sells her body as a sex plaything. In Gomer's case, she seems to have been a slave, owned by someone else who made profit from her filthy living.

But Hosea still loved her. He bought her back out of slavery and took her again into the protection of his home.

In this bitter personal experience Hosea saw a picture of God and God's people. The Lord God loved them and cared for them. Yet they proved faithless and turned away to worship other gods. God still loved them and yearned for them to love him.

Do you see why Hosea's prophecies remind us of Jesus' teachings? Do you see why Hosea's broken home reminds us of Jesus' willingness to pay with his own life so that we can come back into God's household?

ISAIAH

Isaiah is one of the longest and most important books of the Old Testament. It is placed first in the section called Major Prophets, a little past the middle of your Bible.

More than any other Old Testament book, Isaiah looks forward to the coming of Jesus, the Christ or Messiah. No wonder Isaiah is quoted more than four hundred times in the New Testament!

The prophet Isaiah lived in Jerusalem, capital of Judea, the Southern Kingdom. He seems to have been related to both priests and kings. For more than forty years he advised the rulers of Judah. Some took his advice; some refused it, trusting in foreign allies instead of the Lord God. But Isaiah kept on preaching that true safety lay only in obedience to "the Holy One of Israel."

Several ideas about God and God's people stand out more clearly in Isaiah than in any other Old Testament book:

1. There is no God but one. Faithful Israelites had never worshiped any god except the Lord. But they had often thought he was only their special god; other lands had other gods. Isaiah proclaimed the Lord as God of all the earth.

2. The Lord God is holy. Holiness means separation from common things. Isaiah showed that God was holy because he was good and pure, far removed from all sin.

3. God's people must have faith in him. Many parts of Isaiah almost sound like sermons from the New Testament: "Believe! Trust in the Lord!"

4. Even though many of God's people will turn away from him, there will be a faithful minority, or remnant.

At least the first thirty-nine chapters of Isaiah come from times leading up to 587 B.C., when Judah fell to the armies of Babylon. But for eight centuries, Bible scholars have been asking questions about the last part of Isaiah, chapters 40-66: Was it also written before the Jewish people were taken into captivity away from their homeland? Or later?

In Isaiah 8:16, the prophet speaks of "my disciples" as persons who would remember his "testimony" and "teaching." Some people believe that the prophet Isaiah's influence continued for many, many years after his death—that other prophets, inspired by God as Isaiah had been, added to the book that goes by his name. Some people, however, believe that the prophet Isaiah himself wrote the entire book.

Whichever view is correct, it is easy to see that chapters 40-55 of Isaiah mainly speak about the period when the Hebrews were exiles in Babylon. And chapters 56-66 mainly speak about the period when they were again allowed to return to Jerusalem.

Some of the most striking parts of Isaiah are the Servant Songs. These poems, all found in Isaiah 42-53, describe someone who in a special way would be the Servant of the Lord. The most famous of these poems is Isaiah 52:13 to 53:12. Christians through the ages have believed that this prophecy of a suffering Servant was fulfilled in Jesus Christ.

Some of the other prophecies that have been applied to Christ include Isaiah 7:14; 9:2-7; 11:1-9. In your reading from Isaiah, also be sure to include the sublime poetry of chapter 40. If you know the words of Handel's *The Messiah,* you will recognize many familiar verses in Isaiah.

JAMES

James is a short book of the New Testament, placed in order as the second of the General Letters. It is addressed "to the twelve tribes scattered abroad." This may mean all Christians, who are God's new chosen people, replacing the old twelve tribes of Israel. Or it may mean only (or mainly) Jewish Christians.

The "James" who wrote this book nowhere tells us for sure who he is. Most Bible scholars believe, however, that he was the half brother of Jesus, a younger son of Mary and Joseph. He did not become a follower of Christ till after the resurrection. Then he became a leading member of the church in Jerusalem.

It was many years after the book of James was written before all Christians agreed that it should really become a part of the Bible. Even as late as the 1500's, such a great Christian leader as Martin Luther wondered whether it belonged in the Bible.

Most of these questions and doubts have centered around James 2:14-26. Those verses seem at first to contradict what is taught in Paul's Letters. Paul says, "You are saved by faith in Christ, not by good works that you yourself do." James says, "Faith without good works is dead."

Actually, these two ideas are opposite sides of the same coin. The apostle Paul wrote much about what he called "fruits of the Spirit"—that is, good works that Christians are bound to do, if God's Holy Spirit truly lives in them. James only turns this around and looks at the other side: If no one sees any good works in your life, why should anyone think you are really a Christian?

The book of James is one of the hardest in the Bible to outline. It is somewhat like the book of Proverbs. Both seem to be collections of wise sayings and teachings on many matters, strung together in no particular order.

James is a book of action. "How to Act Like a Christian" might be a good title for it. In its 108 verses, there are 54 commands—an average of one command for every two verses!

Although hard to outline, James is not hard to read. You will enjoy its sharply-drawn word pictures—about treating poor people the same as rich people (James 2:1-9); about how hard it is to control one's tongue (3:1-12); about the power of prayer (5:13-17). And don't miss the key verse of the whole book: 1:22.

JEREMIAH

Jeremiah is one of the longest and most important books of the Old Testament. It is placed second in the section called Major Prophets.

No prophet in Bible times had a harder job than Jeremiah. By nature a shy man, he was called to speak boldly before kings, nobles, priests, and crowds of common people. He loved his native land—Judah, the Southern Kingdom. Yet, he had to prophesy that Judah would be destroyed for its wickedness. Even worse, he had to advise repeatedly that the only hope for Judah was to make peace with the Babylonian Empire.

That sounded unpatriotic to Jeremiah's fellow countrymen. It even sounded like treason. Throughout forty years of his ministry, few people would listen to his preaching. Instead, they tried again and again to shut him up—temporarily or permanently.

Jeremiah was called to be a prophet in 626 B.C. He was still prophesying as late as 585 B.C. About 604 B.C., he began to write down his prophecies, with the help of Baruch, his faithful secretary. The first copy was burned up and had to be rewritten.

No one knows how many times the book of Jeremiah was rewritten and added to. It is plain that the book is not arranged in the order things happened. Did this come about because it was put together little by little, with no particular attempt at arrangement? Or is it sorted out more or less by subjects rather than by dates?

Whatever the reason, the jumbled order of Jeremiah makes it hard to outline and confusing to read. But it is worth the effort. Jeremiah's words and actions tell us more about his personality than we know about any other prophet. We can feel what he feels—hurt when he hurts. (For example, read Jeremiah 11:18 to 12:6; 15:10-21; 17:14-18; 18:18-20; 20:7-12.)

Although few people of his own times would listen to Jeremiah's preaching, he cannot be called a failure. A main idea he proclaimed helped prepare the way for the coming of Christ. He spoke of a new agreement or new covenant between God and man. The old covenant had been a group agreement: All of the Israelites had pledged themselves to obey God's laws written on tablets of stone. The new covenant, says Jeremiah, will be an individual matter—an inward commitment (31:31-34).

The outline that follows does not include nearly all of the book of Jeremiah. It only lists, in time order, some of the most interesting events from his life. Be sure to read them!
1. God calls youthful Jeremiah to be his prophet (chapter 1).
2. Jeremiah preaches in the Temple and nearly gets mobbed (26).
3. Jeremiah prophesies in the Temple again, and gets beaten and thrown into the stocks (19:14 to 20:6).
4. Jeremiah fights false prophets—in person and by letter (27-29).
5. Jeremiah dictates a scroll to Baruch and sends him to read it in the Temple; wicked King Jehoiakim destroys it and tries to destroy the men who wrote it; they escape and rewrite it (36).
6. Jeremiah, accused of deserting to the enemy, is thrown into jail (37).
7. An African friend rescues Jeremiah from a dungeon (38).
8. Jerusalem falls to its enemies; Jeremiah's life is spared (39).
9. Jeremiah lives through troubled times after the fall of Jerusalem, and is finally forced into exile in Egypt (40-43).

JOB

Job is an Old Testament book, located just before the middle of the Bible. It is the first in order, and the second in length, of the five books called Poetry.

For a long time Job has been recognized as one of the Bible's most magnificent pieces of literature. Victor Hugo, famous French novelist, called it "perhaps the greatest masterpiece of the human mind." Alfred, Lord Tennyson, outstanding English poet, considered it "the greatest poem of ancient and modern times." Archibald MacLeish, modern American playwright, based his Broadway hit *J. B.* on the book of Job. And the book itself, directly quoted from the Bible, has been adapted into a popular outdoor summer drama.

Like much other great literature, though, Job is not easy to understand. Even when its words are clear, ideas behind the words are sometimes hard to grasp.

The writer of Job (no one knows who he was—or when, or where) asked some big questions. In his day people thought that sorrow, sickness, or loss was always punishment for sin. But in the story of Job, we see a good man who suffers great trouble. Friends come to "comfort" him; instead, they try to get him to admit what a big sinner he really is.

Job answers his friends, but finally turns away from them and directly challenges God: "Why do good people suffer?" he demands. "What does life mean, anyhow? Is God really good?"

God answers Job by showing his great power. And he uses that power to give back even more than Job had lost before—health, wealth, and happiness.

But just a bare telling of the story does not begin to show what riches you will find in the pages of Job. Don't miss magnificent poems about God and nature, such as Job 5:8-16; 12:7-13; 36:26 to 37:24; 38:1 to 39:30; 40:15 to 41:34. Chapter 28 is a beautiful lyric about wisdom. Chapter 29 paints a moving word-picture of the olden days when Job was happy and peaceful as chief of his clan. In Job 31:5-40, Job sets an even higher standard for his own conduct than what the Old Testament laws required.

Be sure to use a modern translation when you read Job. Older versions are hard to understand and often misleading.

JOEL

Joel is the second of twelve short books in the section called Minor Prophets—the last group in the Old Testament.

If any book of the Bible could be called "a book about bugs," Joel comes closest to being that book. The prophet Joel predicted a plague of locusts or grasshoppers. Between these hungry insects and a bad dry spell, the countryside would be ruined.

In this natural disaster the prophet saw a sign of God's working in human affairs. He warned that the locust plague and drouth were as nothing compared to the punishment God would send if sinful people did not turn away from their wickedness.

Almost nothing is known about the prophet Joel. Thirteen people named Joel are mentioned in the Old Testament, but none of them was a prophet. Joel seems to have lived in or near the city of Jerusalem, but no one knows for sure when. He was inspired to write his prophecies in vivid poetry; notice descriptions of the plague of locusts in Joel 1:4,6-7,12; 2:7-8.

An unusual feature of the book of Joel is the number of times it quotes from other Old Testament books. In the seventy-seven verses of Joel there are no less than twenty such quotations.

Joel, in turn, was quoted by Jesus' disciple Simon Peter on a certain famous day. When Peter preached at the first Pentecost Day after Jesus' resurrection, and three thousand people became Christians, Peter's sermon text was Joel 2:28-32. (See Acts 2:16-21.)

One of the most beautiful verses in this short book of prophecy is Joel 2:13.

JOHN

"John" is short for "The Gospel According to John." It is a book of the New Testament—the fourth of four books called Biography.

But John's Gospel, even more so than the other three Gospels, is not a biography in the usual meaning of that word. It does not even mention the birth of its main character.

The purpose of the writer of John is clearly stated in John 20:31: "These are written that you may believe that Jesus is the Christ, the Son of God, and that believing you may have life in his name" (RSV).

There are far greater differences between John's Gospel and the first three Gospels, than there are among any of those three Gospels. About 92 percent of what we read in John is not found in Matthew, Mark, or Luke.

The first three Gospels tell mainly about Jesus' ministry in Galilee; John tells mainly about his ministry in Judea. The first three Gospels do not say much about the passing of time during Jesus' ministry; John makes it plain that Jesus' ministry lasted at least three years. The first three Gospels tell more of what Jesus did; John tells more of what Jesus said about what he did. The first three Gospels give Jesus' teachings to crowds; John gives Jesus' teachings to individuals.

A more basic difference than any of these has to do with the purpose of the writer of the Fourth Gospel, as stated in the verse quoted above. In the first three Gospels, Jesus is careful what he says about his being the Christ or Messiah, and other people only gradually come to realize it. In John's Gospel, Jesus shows himself openly from the beginning as Christ the Son of God, with unlimited power and knowledge.

Yet John's Gospel is actually more alike than different, when compared with Matthew, Mark, and Luke. All four books show that Jesus of Nazareth, a true human being, was also Lord and Christ and Son of God. All four especially seem to come closer together in their later chapters, as they narrate his sufferings, death, and resurrection.

Probably the Fourth Gospel was written many years after the other three. There was no need to repeat all the stories in the first Gospels; instead, the writer of John's Gospel tried to show what those stories meant. He also added other teachings and incidents from Jesus' life that others had not included.

Only John tells about Jesus attending a wedding feast and turning water into wine (2:1-11); about Jesus healing a man beside a pool in Jerusalem (5:1-9); about Jesus restoring sight to a man born blind (9:1-41); about Jesus raising Lazarus from death (11:1-44); about Jesus having a breakfast cookout with seven disciples beside lake Galilee (21:1-14). Only John describes Jesus as the Bread of life (chapter 6), as the Light of the world (8), as the Good Shepherd (10), as the Way and the Truth and the Life (14). And, of course, only John has John 3:16, perhaps the best-known verse in the entire Bible.

Like the other books of Biography, John's Gospel has no author's signature—not even on the earliest copies of it yet found, which date back to A.D. 140. But nearly ever since then, many Christians have believed that the apostle John was the writer. Probably he was the "disciple whom Jesus loved" that is mentioned many times in the book.

1 JOHN

First John is a short book near the back of the New Testament. It is in the section known as General Letters.

Probably "1 John" and "John" are more often confused than any other two books, when a person is trying to find one of them in his Bible. That small number "1" (or the Roman numeral "I" in some Bibles) is easy to overlook in the title.

The books of John and 1 John are alike in that neither one of them is signed by its author. It seems likely that the same person wrote both. Long tradition says that the apostle John was the writer, but this cannot be proved from the Bible itself.

Although 1 John is classified as a "General Letter," it does not begin or end like a letter. There are no personal greetings or messages. Yet it may have been a letter in the sense that it was a sermon or lesson about true Christian beliefs which was circulated among the members of several congregations. Probably these churches were in and around the great city of Ephesus in Asia Minor (now western Turkey).

False teachings were bothering those congregations. The most dangerous one insisted that Jesus had not really come to earth as a genuine human being. He was a god who only play-acted, pretending to live and die and live again. For, according to this false teaching, a god cannot get mixed up with human flesh. Everything on earth is bad; God himself is good.

The apostle John knew better. He knew there is nothing wrong with the human body itself; wrong comes when people use it in sinful ways. And John knew that Jesus had been truly man as well as truly God. In his life and death and resurrection, Jesus showed how all men who believe can come back into a right relationship with God.

The book of 1 John makes clear, then, who Jesus really was. "We saw him; we heard him; we even handled him with our own hands," John stresses. (See 1 John 1:1.) "Anyone who denies that Jesus Christ was both God and man, is like an anti-Christ." (See 1 John 2:22.)

In 1 John 4:8 come those famous words that have so often been quoted: "God is love." Because God is love, explains John, then true followers of God ought to love one another.

2 JOHN

Second John is the shortest book in the entire Bible—only thirteen verses, less than three hundred words. It is in the section called General Letters, near the back of the New Testament.

This little letter is addressed to a woman: "the elect lady and her children." The Greek word translated "elect" means "chosen by God." However, no one is sure exactly how it is used in 2 John.

It may be that the letter was written to a noble Christian lady, describing her as one of God's new chosen people. Or, "the elect lady and her children" may be picture-language for a church—a local congregation with its members.

Bible scholars are no more sure who wrote the letter than they are who received it. The writer only calls himself "the elder." But 2 John sounds so much like 1 John, that both were probably written by the same man. Since early times, many Christians have believed that "the elder" was the apostle John, after he had become an old man living in Ephesus.

Second John was written because "the elder" had found that some of "the elect lady's" children had been following the true commandments of Christ. (Whether this means a certain lady's own children away from home or members of a local church who had moved away, no one can say for sure.) He wrote about his joy because of these "children's" true Christianity. He also warned the lady about false teachers and false teachings—especially the idea that Jesus Christ had not really come to earth as a true human being. "If somebody comes to you teaching this falsehood," the elder warned the lady, "don't even give him the time of day." (See 2 John 10-11.)

The elder finished his letter by explaining that he had much more to tell but wanted to say it in person on a visit. He sent greetings from "the children of your elect sister." (Again, no one knows whether he meant a certain lady's real nephews and nieces, or the members of the church at the place where he was.)

As you read 2 John don't overlook the commandment in verse 5: "Love one another."

3 JOHN

Third John is the second shortest book of the Bible—only a few words longer than 2 John. It is the only book in the Bible with the numeral "3" in its title. Located near the back of the New Testament, it is called one of the General Letters.

This brief letter was written from "the elder" to a Christian named Gaius. The elder (probably the apostle John) complimented Gaius for his hospitality to missionaries and other traveling Christians. "By giving such people room and board in your home," he wrote, "you are taking part in their work." (See 3 John 8.)

Third John also mentions a man named Diotrephes, who was trying to be a dictator in the church. "I'll straighten him out when I come," the elder promised. (See 3 John 9-10.)

Sometimes Christians of today get the idea that everything was always perfect, peaceful, and loving among the earliest Christians. Such books of the Bible as 3 John remind us that Christians are and always have been just ordinary sinful human beings, saved by God's grace.

JONAH

Jonah is one of the shortest books of the Old Testament. It is located in the section called the Minor Prophets.

Most books called "Major Prophets" or "Minor Prophets" mainly contain sermons or prophecies of one or more prophets. Jonah, instead, contains a story about a prophet.

Many people have heard about "Jonah and the whale." Actually, no "whale" is mentioned in Jonah—just some unnamed type of great fish or sea monster. And too much attention to the great fish has kept many people from seeing the book's real message.

Jonah was God's prophet—probably the same one mentioned in 2 Kings 14:25. God sent him to preach in Nineveh, a great and wicked city whose people were enemies of Jonah's nation. Instead, Jonah tried to run away from God. God used a great storm and a great fish to stop him.

Once more God commanded Jonah to go to Nineveh and warn that the city would soon be destroyed because of its wickedness. Dragging his feet, the prophet went. To his surprise, the people of Nineveh listened to his message and turned away from their sins. God responded by having mercy on them and not sending immediate destruction.

Then Jonah got mad. He felt God had made him look like a fool for having warned of a disaster that now would not happen. God could have mercy on the people of Nineveh, but Jonah didn't.

In the last chapter of the book, through the words of God himself, we get the main point of Jonah: "Human beings know what it is to care about the little things of this world—like the plant, Jonah, that shaded you from the hot sun. Why can't you understand, then, that God himself cares about all the peoples of the world?" (See Jonah 4:10-11.)

Some people think that the book of Jonah is literal history. Others think it is an allegory, much like the parables Jesus told.

Either way, the message is the same: Some of God's people long ago—like some of God's people today—thought that God cared only about them, not about other nations. The truth is that God cares about everyone. God's chosen people are chosen not because he loves them more than others, but because he wants them to tell everyone about his love and greatness.

JOSHUA

Joshua is an important book of the Old Testament. It comes first in the section called History.

As you might expect, Joshua is the main character in the book named after him. No one knows who wrote the book; at least parts of it were obviously written long after Joshua's time.

Joshua had been Moses' chief assistant during the long years when the people of Israel had wandered in the desert. God had promised that someday they would take over the land of Canaan and settle down. After Moses died, Joshua, as the Israelites' new leader, became the commander for this military campaign.

The book of Joshua contains exciting stories: how two Israelite spies slipped into an enemy city and nearly got caught (chapter 2); how the Israelites crossed the Jordan River during flood-time (3); how the walls of Jericho fell when Joshua and his men followed strange orders (6).

When you read the bitter, bloody stories in the book of Joshua, you need to remember several things. One is that the natives of Canaan, whom the Israelites nearly wiped out in their brutal attacks, were themselves wild and wicked people. Their religion included sacrificing children, worshiping snakes, and abusing their own bodies sexually. No wonder the Israelites felt God wanted them to slaughter the Canaanites!

But another thing to remember is this: The Israelites themselves did not have as clear an understanding of God, and of God's will for man, as Christians can have today. God's love shown in the Lord Jesus Christ should make a difference in the way you read and understand this history of savage ancient times.

This simple outline shows General Joshua's battle plan:
1. Joshua leads the Israelites to conquer most of Canaan (chapters 1-12).
    (1) They get ready to fight (1-5).
    (2) They conquer central Canaan, cutting the land in two (6-9).
    (3) They conquer southern Canaan (10).
    (4) They conquer northern Canaan (11).
    (5) Chapter 12 gives a summary of the Israelites' victories.
2. The Israelites divide the land and begin to settle it (13-22).
3. Joshua reminds the Israelites to remain true to God (23-24).

JUDE

Jude is one of the shortest (only one chapter of twenty-five verses) and strangest books of the New Testament. It is placed in the group of books called General Letters and is the next to last book in the Bible.

The "Jude" who wrote this little letter may have been Jesus' half brother, a younger son of Mary and Joseph. Two of Jesus' twelve disciples were also named Jude or Judas. But the "Jude" who wrote this book may instead have been a Christian of somewhat later times, who lived after the first apostles had all (or nearly all) died; notice what he said in verse 17.

Two things make Jude a rather strange book. One is the apparent fact that either Jude is a shortened version of 2 Peter or 2 Peter is a lengthened version of Jude. The two letters seem too much alike for this to have been a coincidence. The other strange thing about Jude is that it quotes from two books that are not in the Bible, almost as if they were part of the Scriptures. (See Jude verses 9 and 14-15.)

The book of Jude is a fierce attack on certain persons, calling themselves Christians, who were teaching false beliefs. They were claiming that Christ could not have been a real human being because the spirit is good but the body is evil. Because they thought the body was evil anyway, they could see nothing wrong with abusing it in sinful ways.

In order to stand firm against such mistaken ideas, Jude called on his fellow Christians to hold fast to "the faith which was once for all delivered to the saints" (Jude verse 3) and to keep themselves "in the love of God" (verse 21).

The most memorable part of the book of Jude is found in its last two verses. This strange little letter ends with as beautiful a benediction as you can find anywhere in the Bible.

JUDGES

"Judges" is one of the most misleading titles of any Bible book. For modern readers, a title such as "Heroes" or "Chieftains" would come closer to the truth. Judges is the second book in the second section of the Old Testament—the books called History.

The book of Joshua, which comes just before Judges, tells how Joshua led the Israelites to invade the land of Canaan. But they did not conquer all of it. Each tribe still had to clear out pockets of resistance in the area where they settled.

Judges tells how the Israelites, in times of peace and success, would forget God and worship idols. God would punish them by allowing enemies to defeat and enslave them. When they would turn back to the true God again, he would raise up a new champion who was to lead them to victory once more.

Some of these heroes also acted as judges when peacetime came after war. Few if any of them led all of the Israelites at the same time. Probably each ruled only one area; so more than one chieftain might have lived during the same period of time.

The judges were not all good and wise men. Jephthah made a human sacrifice of his only daughter. Gideon set up an idol. Abimelech slaughtered his own brothers. Samson misused his great strength to follow whatever lusty whim came into his mind. Yet the book of Judges shows how God could use even such men as these to work his will on earth.

This outline will help you find their stories:
1. Review of times up to Joshua's death (Judges 1:1 to 2:10).
2. Summary of the entire book of Judges (2:11 to 3:6).
3. Stories of the judges (3:7 to 16:31).
    (1) Three early judges (3:7-31).
    (2) Deborah and Barak (4-5).
    (3) Gideon (6-8).
    (4) Abimelech (9).
    (5) Two less important judges (10:1-5).
    (6) Jephthah (10:6 to 12:7).
    (7) Three less important judges (12:8-15).
    (8) Samson (13-16).
4. Migration of the tribe of Dan (17-18).
5. Wrongdoing and punishment of the tribe of Benjamin (19-21).

1 KINGS

First Kings is a book of the Old Testament, located in about the middle of the section called History. The Hebrew Bible made 1 Kings and 2 Kings just one long book. In the first Bible translation ever prepared, the Greek Old Testament, this history was first divided into two books.

It is not hard to guess from the title what the book of 1 Kings is about: kings—lots of them. The purpose or theme of the book is harder to guess, though; it is not just a straight royal history.

The author of 1 Kings (no one knows who he was) was inspired by God to write history for spiritual reasons. He knew that the Lord God had made a special promise or covenant with the people of Israel: He would be their God, and would bless them, if they would be faithful and obedient to him.

This unknown writer studied other books about the times of the kings. (Some of these source books he mentions; see, for instance, 1 Kings 11:41; 14:19,29.) As he did so, he began to realize that very few of the rulers of his people had been true to God.

In writing his nation's history, this author judged each king by one standard alone: whether that monarch was faithful to God. Nothing else really seemed to matter. Omri was one of the most powerful and successful of all kings. But the book of 1 Kings dismisses him with just ten verses (1 Kings 16:16-17,21-28) because he did not keep God's covenant.

The first eleven chapters of 1 Kings tell about the reign of Solomon, David's son. Included are accounts of how the great Temple was built in Jerusalem, and of how the Queen of Sheba came from far away in Africa to see for herself whether Solomon was as great as she had been told.

Beginning in 1 Kings, chapter 12, you can read how Solomon's foolish son King Rehoboam muffed his own chance at greatness. His kingdom split into two nations that were longtime rivals.

The two most striking characters in 1 Kings are the fiery prophet Elijah and his great enemy, the brave but wicked King Ahab. Throughout the last seven chapters of the book (beginning at 1 Kings 16:29) their stories are intertwined. And don't miss the point of Elijah's heroic stand: Only the Lord is God. All men—including kings—must serve and worship him.

2 KINGS

Second Kings is placed near the middle of the section of
Old Testament books called History. In early times it and 1 Kings
were combined; later they were divided into two books.

The title of 2 Kings shows what kind of people it is about.
Yet, one of the most interesting characters in it is not a king but
a prophet.

Chapters 1 and 2 of 2 Kings tell about the last years of the
fiery old prophet Elijah. As his successor he picked a young man
named Elisha. Stories about the prophet Elisha are woven together
with stories about kings, throughout the entire first half of the
book of 2 Kings.

But people other than kings and prophets appear in those
stories, too. Don't miss reading about the kindhearted Shunammite
woman in chapter 4; about the sick Syrian general in chapter
5; about the lepers who made a great discovery in chapter 7.

Second Kings, chapters 9-11, tell one of the most violent series
of events in all the bloody history of Old Testament times. An
army commander named Jehu, encouraged by the prophet Elisha,
led a rebellion against his master. He wiped out the descendants
of wicked King Ahab, including two monarchs murdered on the
same day. In all the confusion a cruel queen seized power by
killing her own grandsons. Finally she too died horribly.

Down to chapter 17, 2 Kings records the history of two rival
nations: Israel, the Northern Kingdom, and Judah, the Southern
Kingdom. All of the kings of Israel were bad, according to the
view of the writer of 2 Kings, because all of them were untrue
to God and God's covenant, or special promise-relationship, with
his Chosen People. Finally in 721 B.C. the Northern Kingdom
was destroyed by the Assyrian Empire.

The rest of 2 Kings, chapters 18-25, tells about the last years
of Judah, the Southern Kingdom. Under good kings such as
Hezekiah and Josiah, it still enjoyed some years of greatness. But
most of its kings, too, were bad. Finally Judah was conquered
by the Babylonian Empire in 587 B.C.

Second Kings contains exciting adventures; it does not contain
many helpful teachings. But its main message is clear: Failure
to trust in God brings disaster—even for men on thrones.

LAMENTATIONS

Lamentations is one of the shorter Old Testament books. It is placed in the middle of the section called Major Prophets. Actually, however, it belongs with the group of books called Poetry because each of its five chapters is a separate poem.

"Lamentations" means "sad songs." Each of the five poems mourns the destruction of Jerusalem by enemy armies in 587 B.C. The first Bible translation ever made, the Greek Old Testament, started the custom of putting Lamentations right after Jeremiah. There is no reason to believe that people before then (the third century B.C.) thought Jeremiah wrote these poems, because in the Hebrew Bible the book was not placed with Jeremiah.

Some of the descriptions in Lamentations are so vivid you can see and hear and feel that long-ago time of sorrow and disaster. Four of the five poems are acrostics, using lines or stanzas that begin with the twenty-two letters of the Hebrew alphabet, in proper order. And Lamentations 3:22-24 is as lovely a statement of trust in God as you can find anywhere in the Scriptures.

LEVITICUS

Leviticus is the third book of the Bible, and of the Old Testament section called Law. Its title comes from the name of the tribe of Levi; members of this Israelite tribe became priests for God's Chosen People in olden times. And Leviticus has more to say about priests, sacrifices, and laws than any other book.

Perhaps Leviticus has marked the breaking of more Bible-reading resolutions than any other book, too. When a person resolves to read the entire Bible, he naturally starts with Genesis, the first book. Genesis contains interesting stories that make for easy reading. So does Exodus, the second book. Only in the later chapters of Exodus might a well-meaning reader start to bog down in details about priests and laws. When he hits Leviticus and finds it almost entirely made up of such material, he may abandon Bible-reading as a bad job!

This is a pity, for Leviticus—like all Bible books—has its message, or God would not have inspired men to write and keep such a book. The keynote of Leviticus is found in chapter 20, verse 26: "Ye shall be holy unto me; for I the Lord am holy, and have severed you from other people, that ye should be mine."

The Israelites, like people of today, lived in a wicked world. But most other tribes and nations believed that their gods were just as wicked as they were, so what difference did it make how they behaved? It was a new idea in the world that the Lord, the God of Israel, was holy and pure. What was more, he insisted that his people should also be holy and pure.

Chapters 1-16 of Leviticus describe in detail how sinful people could approach a holy God: through sacrifice. The Hebrew word for sacrifice comes from a word that means "to draw near." By giving offerings of what they had raised in their fields or nurtured in their flocks, the Israelites showed that they were devoted to God.

Chapters 17-27 of Leviticus tell how God's people can go on living in right relationship with him—how they can become holy because God is holy. Rules listed in these chapters range all the way from proper sexual conduct to kind treatment of handicapped persons. Included also is a verse Jesus quoted: "You shall love your neighbor as yourself" (Leviticus 19:18, RSV).

LUKE

Luke is the longest book of the New Testament—not in number of chapters, but in actual content. It is the third of four books placed in the section called Biography, or Gospels. Its full title is "The Gospel According to Luke."

More so than any of the other three Gospels, the book of Luke truly does set out to tell the life story of Jesus Christ, in the usual meaning of the word "biography." It begins with important events leading up to his birth, and ends with important events just after his death: that is, his resurrection and ascension.

Actually, Luke is Volume 1 of a two-volume work. Its sequel is the book of Acts, which was written by the same man and continues the story of Jesus' early followers.

The writer, Dr. Luke, was not among those early followers himself. As far as anyone knows, he did not become a Christian until the times when the apostle Paul was making his missionary journeys, many years later. Probably Luke was a Greek, not a Jew. This makes him most likely the only Gentile (non-Jew) who was inspired to write a part of the Bible. And his part was an important one.

In the first few verses of his Gospel, Luke states how he went about preparing his biography of Jesus. Others had already written such books—probably Mark and Matthew among them. But Luke also talked with "those who from the beginning were eyewitnesses" (Luke 1:2, RSV).

Guided by God as he pulled all his sources together, this Greek physician produced the most complete biography of Jesus in existence. He repeated much that is also told in Matthew and in Mark. But fully 50 percent of Luke's Gospel is not found in any other book of the Bible.

Stories of Jesus' birth and childhood, for instance: Mary's visit to her cousin Elizabeth, the birth of John the Baptist, the holy Babe in the manger, the shepherds, old Simeon and Anna in the Temple, the boy Jesus making a trip to Jerusalem at the age of twelve—all of these are recorded nowhere except in Luke. Probably Luke learned about them in conversations with Mary.

Stories Jesus himself told: the good Samaritan (Luke 10:25-37), the prodigal son (Luke 15:11-32), the rich man and the beggar

Lazarus (Luke 16:19-31)—these are some of the parables related by Luke alone.

Luke's Gospel is different from the others in several ways. Here are some of those differences: (1) Jesus is shown more clearly as both *man* and God, able to feel and react as other human beings. (2) Jesus is shown more clearly as the *Savior for everyone*—Jew and Gentile, rich and poor, young and old. (3) More is told about the *prayers* of Jesus. (4) More is told about *women* whom Jesus helped or who became Jesus' followers. (5) More use is made of *praise poems* that Christians have been singing since ancient times: Mary's Magnificat in Luke 1:46-55, for instance, and the angels' Gloria in Luke 2:14.

This simple outline will help you study Luke:
1. Jesus' early life (Luke 1:1 to 4:13).
2. Jesus' ministry in Galilee (4:14 to 9:50).
3. Jesus' journey from Galilee to Jerusalem (9:51 to 19:27).
4. Jesus' last days in Jerusalem—his sufferings, death, and burial (19:28 to 23:56).
5. Jesus' resurrection, appearances to his followers, and return to heaven (24:1-53).

MALACHI

Malachi is the last book of the Old Testament and also the last of the twelve short books grouped as Minor Prophets.

No one knows much about the prophet Malachi. Even his very name may not have been a name at all, only a title, since it means "my messenger." (Notice Malachi 3:1.) Whoever the writer was, he lived in a late period of Old Testament history. The defeated Israelites had been carried away into exile. Then some of them had been allowed to return. Jerusalem had been rebuilt, along with its new Temple of the Lord God.

Yet, things did not seem to be going well with the Israelites. They were not enjoying the power and prosperity their ancestors had known long ago. Many of them decided that their religion had no real meaning. Therefore, they just play-acted, going through the motions of worship. Even priests no longer respected the Lord and his laws.

Malachi spoke sternly against this state of affairs. "Better to lock up the Temple," he fumed, "than to go on as you are doing!" (See Malachi 1:10.)

The style of Malachi's prophecy is different from that of any other book. He wrote in questions and answers, as if God were arguing with his people. Here are some of Malachi's questions:

"What proof is there that God loves us?" (Malachi 1:2-5.)
"In what ways have we failed to honor God?" (1:6 to 2:9.)
"Why doesn't God accept our worship?" (2:10-16.)
"How have we wearied God's patience?" (2:17 to 3:6.)
"How can we return to God?" (3:7-12.)
"In what ways have we spoken against God?" (3:13 to 4:3.)
Two other unusual features of Malachi are these:

1. It includes a clear call about giving to God's service at least a tithe (one tenth) of all that we have. (Read 3:8-10.)

2. It includes the only prophecy in the Old Testament that someone will come before the promised Messiah, to prepare the way for him. (See Malachi 3:1-4; 4:5-6.) This forerunner of the Christ will be a rough, fierce man—like the prophet Elijah come to earth again. Malachi's prophecy was fulfilled in the coming of John the Baptist. (See Matthew 17:10-13; Luke 7:24-27.)

MARK

Mark is the second book of the New Testament. It is the shortest of four books in the section called Biography. Its proper title is "The Gospel According to Mark."

Why are there four Gospels? Many events in Bible times are told more than once. But only the life of our Lord Jesus Christ has four separate and distinct tellings. This shows that who he was and what he did and said is more important than anything else.

Also, each of the four Gospels is written from a different point of view. Each tells about Jesus in a way not found in the others. All four are needed to complete the picture.

Matthew, Mark, and Luke are often called the Synoptic Gospels. "Synoptic" means "seeing with the same eyes." The main order of happenings in these three is much more alike, than any one of the three is like the Fourth Gospel, John. Many Bible scholars think the similarity of Matthew, Mark, and Luke has a simple cause. They believe that Mark was the first person inspired by God to write down an account of Jesus' life, and that Matthew and Luke used this basic record in their inspired books.

Mark (his full name was John Mark) is mentioned several times in other books of the New Testament. He was a missionary, working sometimes with Paul, sometimes with Peter. From earliest times many Christians have thought that Mark got his main information about Jesus from the apostle Peter.

Mark's Gospel makes lively reading. He didn't worry about careful literary style; he was in too much of a hurry for that. More than forty times in sixteen chapters he used a Greek word that means "immediately." His narrative leaps from one happening to the next, telling much more of what Jesus did than of what Jesus said. In passages that are also found in Matthew or Luke or both, it is Mark who often gives little vivid details that help us see, hear, and feel what was going on.

Although John Mark himself was a Jew, he seems to have spent most of his life among non-Jewish people. Probably his biography of Jesus was slanted toward Romans, conquerors of the known world in their day. So Mark didn't bother much about Jewish matters. He didn't even use that favorite Jewish word, "law." What few Jewish words and customs he mentioned are carefully explained for readers who might be puzzled by them.

Mark emphasized the power of Jesus Christ—ruling winds and waves, healing the sick, raising the dead. Such a mighty Messiah could break from his tomb and come out a living Lord forevermore. Even proud Romans should bow to such a victorious Savior! Here is a brief outline of this fast-moving book:

1. John the Baptist and Jesus himself prepare for Jesus' ministry (Mark 1:1-13).
2. Jesus ministers publicly with great power (1:14 to 3:12).
3. Jesus begins to withdraw from the crowds to teach his disciples, occasionally appearing in public again (3:13 to 8:30).
4. Jesus begins to predict how his life will end, while continuing to meet human needs and to train his disciples (8:31 to 10:52).
5. Jesus spends his final week in Jerusalem (11:1 to 15:47).
6. Jesus rises in power from the grave (16:1-8).

(Other verses, 9-20, that appear at the end of Mark in most Bibles, are not found in the earliest copies of that book. No one knows when or by whom they were added, or whether Mark's own ending to his Gospel has been lost.)

MATTHEW

Matthew is the first book of the New Testament. It has the most chapters, but is second in actual length, among four books called Biography, or Gospels.

The first chapter of this first book has often bothered people who set out to read the entire New Testament. Certainly it isn't very interesting to plow through seventeen verses of family trees. Yet, this first section of Matthew's Gospel is especially important when we understand the purpose of the book: to show that Jesus of Nazareth was indeed the Christ, the promised Messiah, the Savior sent from God in fulfilment of Old Testament prophecies. Matthew 1:1-17 shows that Jesus' family line could be traced down from Abraham, Isaac, and Jacob, the Hebrew founding fathers, through the great King David and his successors. In every way Jesus met the requirements for the Christ, the everlasting King.

About 90 percent of what is related in Mark's Gospel, is retold in Matthew's Gospel. For this and other reasons, many people believe that Mark was written earlier and that the author of Matthew was inspired to make use of that book in his own preparation. But Matthew is far from a carbon copy of Mark.

Nowhere does the author of the first Gospel tell us who he is. But since earliest Christian times there have been traditions that he was Matthew—a hated, thieving tax-collector whom Jesus changed and called to become one of his disciples. As a skilful clerk and office worker, Matthew would have practiced keeping careful records. This ability shows up in the biography he wrote of Jesus.

Matthew tells us more of what Jesus *said* than does any other source. If you have a Bible in which Jesus' words are printed in red letters, you may have noticed that Matthew is "redder" than the other three Gospels. Over 60 percent of all the verses in Matthew contain direct quotations from Jesus.

Matthew recorded long sermons or teachings from Jesus' lips. The best-known one is usually called the Sermon on the Mount (Matthew 5-7). Others are in chapters 10; 13; 18; 23; and 24-25.

Many of Jesus' actions, which Mark also recorded, were rearranged by Matthew according to subject or logical order. He also added stories about Jesus found nowhere else; the Wise Men and the star is perhaps the most famous of these (Matthew 2).

Above all, Matthew made sure his readers would agree that Jesus was the promised Christ. He quoted from the Old Testament more than any of the other Gospel-writers. Some Bible scholars believe that Matthew even arranged his book in five great sections, deliberately imitating the five books of Law that begin the Old Testament.

Matthew, then, is a bridge-book. Perhaps it was placed first in the arrangement of New Testament books because Christians of early times thought that it (not Mark) was the first Gospel written. Be that as it may, Matthew fits in the place where it was put. It makes a proper link between the Old Testament and the New—between prophecy and fulfilment of prophecy.

Read all of Matthew. Jesus' spoken words are full of lively stories, of down-to-earth advice, of heavenly teachings compared to earthly things such as goats and sheep, grapes and figs, gates and lamps, salt and sand. Perhaps no Bible book is better suited as a manual for Christians to follow in their daily lives.

MICAH

Micah is a book of the Old Testament, located just before the middle of the last section, the Minor Prophets.

This book is a good example of what a person can miss if he skips or passes lightly over the Minor Prophets in reading the Bible. Its seven chapters tell no interesting stories like those found in Jonah or Amos. At a glance, it appears to be just one more short book among twelve—five before it, six after it, with little to mark one as being different from another. Yet Micah actually contains some of the most important and most beautiful verses in the entire Bible.

The prophet Micah was not a city man. He lived in a rural village during the eighth century B.C. In those times enemy armies often rampaged through the countryside of Judah, the Southern Kingdom. When foreign looters stayed home, the poor peasants were not much better off because cruel kings and crooked priests in Jerusalem took all they could get away with.

Micah was not one to keep quiet about such matters. In the first three chapters of his book are some of the hottest words found anywhere in the Old Testament. Northern Kingdom, Southern Kingdom—both were filled with wickedness and would be punished by God, thundered this inspired peasant-prophet. His prediction that Temple hill in Jerusalem would become like a plowed-up field, was still being quoted in that doomed city a century later. (See Micah 3:12 and Jeremiah 26:16-19.)

But there was still hope for the future. In later chapters Micah predicts the coming of the Messiah. Micah 5:2 even adds the detail that he would be born in Bethlehem. (This is perhaps the single most important exact prediction that is recorded in the Old Testament and fulfilled in the New.) Micah 4:1-7 gives a lovely word-picture of the Messiah's future reign. Micah 6:6-8 and 7:7-8,18-20 are also gems of poetic truth. Here is 6:8 in the Revised Standard Version.

> He has showed you, O man, what is good;
>   And what does the Lord require of you
> But to do justice, and to love kindness,
>   And to walk humbly with your God?

NAHUM

Nahum is a short book located just past the middle of the last section in the Old Testament, the Minor Prophets. Like most prophetic books, it is named after the prophet who apparently was inspired to write it. The word "Nahum" means "comfort." But the message of the book's three brief chapters is anything but comfort—for enemies of God and of God's Chosen People.

In the eighth and seventh centuries before Christ, the Assyrian Empire seemed absolutely unbeatable. Nation after nation fell before its conquering armies. Israel, the Northern Kingdom, held one of the strongest fortresses anywhere: Samaria, its capital city. Yet the Assyrians had captured Samaria, about a hundred years before the times of the prophet Nahum.

It was not just that the Assyrians were so powerful. They were also proud and cruel. Their prisoners were often tortured to death, just for the fun of it.

Little Judah, the Southern Kingdom, seemed several times next on the list to be gobbled up by this haughty foe that strutted across the world. But Nahum the prophet thought otherwise. God inspired him to predict that mighty Nineveh, capital of Assyria, would soon be destroyed.

Nineveh sat on riverbanks, safe behind battlements fifty feet high. But in the year 612 B.C., a sudden rise in the water level flooded Nineveh and dissolved its sun-hardened mud-brick walls. Read Nahum for a fiercely vivid description of the bloody scenes that followed.

Maybe there is some "comfort" in Nahum after all. It helps a little in hard times to know that God will sooner or later punish the wicked and the cruel of this world.

NEHEMIAH

Nehemiah is an important book of the Old Testament. It is placed next to last among the twelve books grouped as History.

The book of Nehemiah brings the history of God's Chosen People down to a later date than any other book of the Old Testament: about 445 to 425 B.C. No one knows who was inspired by God to write the book, but whoever he was, it is plain that he had access to a first-person account from Nehemiah himself.

Nehemiah is one of the most underrated heroes in the Bible. A high official at the court of the Persian king, he chose to take his life in his hands by asking for a hard mission. Some of his fellow Jewish exiles had been allowed to return to Jerusalem. But they were bothered by marauders because the city had no walls.

Appointed governor by the king, Nehemiah hurried to Jerusalem. By night he made a secret trip of inspection around the ruined city. Then he challenged the people to begin rebuilding.

More trouble followed. Enemies used plots, mockery, false reports, double agents, and bald-faced threats to try to stop the construction project. Nehemiah kept on, even when his workmen had to build with weapons in one hand and tools in the other. In just fifty-two days the job was finished.

With the city now secure, Nehemiah turned to other matters. He encouraged Ezra the scribe (the same one told about in the Bible book by that name) to teach the people God's laws. He also straightened out such wrongs as mistreatment of the poor, neglect of the Temple, and failure to keep the Lord's Day holy.

This partial outline of Nehemiah deliberately leaves out some sections that are mainly lists of names:
1. Nehemiah leads in rebuilding the wall (chapters 1-6).
   (1) Nehemiah hears bad news from Jerusalem (1).
   (2) Nehemiah goes to Jerusalem and starts work (2).
   (3) Enemies try to stop the work (4).
   (4) Nehemiah stops mistreatment of the poor (5).
   (5) The wall is finished in spite of opposition (6).
2. Nehemiah leads in other matters (7-13).
   (1) Ezra teaches and renews promises to God (8-9; 10:28-39).
   (2) Princes, priests, and Levites dedicate the wall (12:27-47).
   (3) Nehemiah corrects several wrongs (13:4-22).

NUMBERS

Numbers is the fourth book of the Bible. It is the second longest of five books in the Law section of the Old Testament.

In the Hebrew Bible, Numbers is entitled "In the Wilderness." This seems a better name for the book. It takes up the story of the Israelites (as told in the book of Exodus) after they had received the Ten Commandments at Mount Sinai, and tells what happened to them during forty years of wandering in the wilderness.

Yet "Numbers" isn't a bad title, either. This name comes from the fact that the Israelites took a census twice—once at the beginning of that forty-year period, again near the end of it.

Numbers does not try to tell nearly everything that happened during the forty years. In fact, it seems at first glance to be a strange mixture of historical records, laws, stories, poems, and prophecies—some spoken by a man who was not a prophet of God.

Yet, the materials that make up Numbers were selected with a purpose. God inspired the writer or writers (Moses or whoever it may have been) to include materials that showed how the Lord was training his Chosen People. The Israelites left Egypt as an undisciplined mob, newly freed from slavery. They entered the Promised Land forty years later as an army, ready to fight at God's command. Numbers tells how God led them through this long period of preparation.

This list will help you find some of the more interesting parts of the book of Numbers:
1. Aaron's beautiful benediction (Numbers 6:22-27).
2. How the Israelites traveled (9:15 to 10:6; 10:11-13,33-36).
3. How the Israelites got food in the wilderness (11:1-35).
4 Miriam's complaint against her brother Moses (12:1-16).
5. The story of the twelve spies, their two reports which did not agree, and what happened when the Israelites believed the wrong report (13:1-3; 13:17 to 14:45).
6. A rebellion against Moses and Aaron's leadership (16:1 to 17:11).
7. Adventures on the way to the Promised Land (20:1 to 21:35).
8. The strange story of Balak and Balaam (22:1 to 24:25).
9. Moses' successor, Joshua (27:12-23).
10. A special agreement with two of the Israelite tribes (32:1-33).

OBADIAH

Obadiah is the shortest book of the Old Testament—only one chapter of twenty-one verses. It is located fourth among twelve short books that make up the last section of the Old Testament, the Minor Prophets.

Do you remember the story of Jacob and Esau, twins who became rivals? Even though they did not always get along with each other, yet they were blood brothers. It would seem, therefore, that the Israelites (descended from Jacob) and the Edomites (descended from Esau) should have been friendly tribes. As a matter of fact, they were more often than not at war with each other.

At some time in the history of the Israelites, the Edomites helped foreign enemies conquer Jerusalem. This may have been when that city was destroyed by Babylonian armies in 587 B.C.; or perhaps it was some other event.

The Edomites themselves thought they would never suffer the fate of their Israelite cousins. From their high, rocky fortresses they could laugh at their enemies down below.

The prophet Obadiah saw the wrong in this state of affairs. In his little book of prophecy, he told how even the proud Edomites would be hauled down in defeat, like an eagle pulled from its mountain nest. (Notice verses 3-4.) And that is just what happened to the Edomites, not too many years after the fall of Jerusalem.

No one knows anything more than this about the prophet Obadiah. A dozen other Obadiah's are mentioned in the Old Testament, but there is no reason to think that any one of them was the man inspired by God to write this brief warning to enemies of God's Chosen People.

1 PETER

First Peter is a book located in the next to last section of the New Testament, the General Letters. It was addressed to Christians in Asia Minor (now Turkey). According to 1 Peter 5:13, Simon Peter wrote his letter from "Babylon." This, however, was more than likely a sort of code name for Rome; both were great, wicked capital cities. And Peter had good reason for using code.

Christians were being persecuted in those days. Many Bible scholars think 1 Peter was written during the reign of Nero. This mad Roman emperor burned Christians every night to give light for such "games" as throwing other Christians to hungry lions. No wonder there are no less than seven different Greek words that mean "suffering" in the five chapters of 1 Peter!

Simon Peter urged his fellow believers to stand firm in the midst of sufferings. He reminded them of the example of the Lord Jesus: 1 Peter 2:21-25 makes a beautiful commentary on Isaiah 53, which prophesies the sufferings of Christ.

2 PETER

Second Peter is a short book of the New Testament. It is in the section called General Letters.

Reading 2 Peter, especially such favorite verses as those found in 1:16-21 or in 3:18, you would never guess what a strange history this letter has had. No book of the Bible has had a harder time being accepted as a genuine part of the inspired Word of God. It was the last book to be added to the list of twenty-seven books that we now call the New Testament. No Christian even mentioned 2 Peter in his writings till about A.D. 250, and then only to say that not everyone recognized it as Scripture.

Three things especially have bothered Christians through the centuries about 2 Peter: (1) It seems so very different from 1 Peter, which was supposed to have been written by the same man. (2) It seems so much like the book of Jude, especially 2 Peter 2. (3) It mentions Paul's Letters as if they were already considered a part of the Bible. (See 2 Peter 3:15-16.)

Of course the apostle Peter, like the apostle Paul, sometimes used secretaries to help him write his letters. Silas, or Silvanus, was Peter's secretary for his first letter (see 1 Peter 5:12), and maybe it was he who finished up the exact wording of it. This would help explain why 2 Peter seems so different from 1 Peter—if Peter used a different secretary or wrote the later letter directly himself.

No one knows for sure how to solve the puzzle about the book of Jude and 2 Peter 2. But remember: Questions as to who really wrote a Bible book, or when or why it was written, or how it finally got into the Bible, do not decide the value of that book for Christians today. Second Peter 1:20-21 is itself a good reminder that God has many ways of working—through many men in many ages. And it is first of all *God's* Word that you are reading—not Peter's or anybody else's.

Second Peter can be rather neatly outlined. Each of its three chapters has one main piece of advice for Christians of all generations:
1. Grow as a Christian! (chapter 1.)
2. Watch out for false teachers! (2.)
3. Wait patiently for the second coming of our Lord! (3.)

PHILEMON

Philemon is the last in order and shortest in length of thirteen New Testament books called Paul's Letters. It is the only example in the Bible of a personal letter written by the apostle Paul.

While Paul was a prisoner in Rome, about A.D. 61-62, he met a young runaway slave named Onesimus, and led him to become a follower of the Lord Jesus Christ. (Paul mentions Onesimus in Colossians 4:9.)

Fortunately for the youthful slave, his owner was a friend of Paul's—a Christian in Colossae named Philemon. Onesimus had apparently stolen something from his master when he ran away. Philemon could legally punish him by torture or death. But Paul felt sure Philemon would accept Onesimus as a new Christian brother when he understood the situation. So Paul wrote his briefest letter to explain the matter to his friend.

Paul did not flatly tell Philemon what to do, although he felt he had a right to do so (notice verses 8-10). Instead, he smoothly and tactfully suggested how he believed Philemon would want to treat Onesimus, after reading Paul's note.

PHILIPPIANS

Philippians is a short book of the New Testament, located about the middle of the group identified as Paul's Letters.

Several times during Paul's checkered life, he was thrown into prison for preaching the good news about Jesus Christ. During one of these imprisonments, he welcomed a visitor from Philippi named Epaphroditus. Lydia and the jailer at Philippi and other Christians there (you can read about them in Acts 16) had heard about Paul's troubles. They had sent Paul their love by Epaphroditus and had also sent a gift of money.

The messenger from Philippi had planned to stay with Paul. But he became dangerously ill, so that both he and Paul thought he had better go back home again. With him Paul sent the letter we call Philippians.

Many of Paul's Letters sound like arguments . . . and they are. Many of them were written to attack false beliefs or to settle troubles in the Christian community. The church at Philippi, compared to other early groups of Christians, had no such problems. There were a couple of lady members who sometimes irritated each other; there were a few doubts, a few grumblings—but no serious difficulties. Therefore, Philippians breathes a spirit of joy not found in any of Paul's other letters.

Paul wrote to thank his friends in Philippi. He told them how even his imprisonment had helped to spread the gospel. He sent them news about other Christian friends. And he gave them good advice, as their spiritual father.

Philippians is perhaps the hardest to outline of all Paul's Letters. Because he was writing a relaxed, happy message to friends, Paul let his mind skip from one idea to another. Important teachings about the Christian faith, practical counsel about the Christian life, personal notes—all are mixed up together. Yet, in the midst of all this, Paul included the clearest statement anywhere in the Bible of the fact that Christ, the eternal all-powerful Son of God, deliberately emptied himself of his heavenly glory to become a man and the Savior of all men (2:5-11).

Don't leave any of Philippians out of your Bible study. It is much easier to read than to outline. Take time to memorize a few verses as you go—maybe 1:21; 3:14; 4:4,6-8,13,19-20.

PROVERBS

Proverbs is an Old Testament book of Poetry, located just after Psalms near the middle of the Bible.

Proverbs 1:1 states that Solomon was one of the authors of the book. But he wasn't the only one. Other verses mention other authors—such as Agur (Proverbs 30:1) and Lemuel (Proverbs 31:1). Parts of the book were put into writing, or were collected and arranged, by scribes working for King Hezekiah, Solomon's many-great's-grandson (Proverbs 25:1).

The book of Proverbs, then, represents the inspired wisdom of many men in many ages. Probably it was gradually put together into the form that we know today.

Sometimes Proverbs (like Job and Ecclesiastes) is called "wisdom literature." This is a good description of it. Proverbs gives much good advice about wise ways of thinking and acting. But more important than this, it tells that a wise head with a wicked heart does not actually make a person wise at all. The key verse of the entire book is Proverbs 1:7a: "The fear of the Lord is the beginning of knowledge."

One unusual feature of Proverbs is that "wisdom" is often pictured as a wise woman teacher. She invites foolish youngsters to come to her school and learn. (Notice Proverbs 1:20-23; 3:13-18; 7:1-4; 8:1 to 9:6.) Another unusual section is found at the very end of the book: a beautiful portrait in poetry of an ideal wife and mother (31:10-31).

Many sections of Proverbs—chapters 10-15, for instance—are made up of just what you would expect from the title of this book. Each verse is a separate "proverb"—a short, wise saying, easy to remember; an important truth in a few pointed words.

Proverbs can be outlined according to groupings stated by the book itself—which chapters came from Solomon, which from Hezekiah's scribes, and so on. But such an outline would not really tell you much about what is in those chapters.

Perhaps more than any other book of the Bible, Proverbs can be read starting just anywhere—back, front, or middle. Open it where you please, and begin reading. So you happened to hit a less interesting section? Keep on reading; in a few more verses it will change the subject!

PSALMS

Psalms is the longest book of the Bible, located exactly in the middle of it. It is grouped in the Poetry section of the Old Testament.

The word "psalms" means "songs accompanied by stringed instruments." In the Hebrew Bible this book has another title, which means "songs of praise." Either way, Psalms is a hymnbook.

Recent translations of the Bible show that all 150 of the psalms are written in poetic lines. These poems do not rhyme—not even in the original Hebrew language of the Old Testament—but they do have noticeable rhythm. Often they repeat key words and key ideas to drive home meaning or mood.

Who wrote these many songs? At first glance the answer seems easy. Almost half of them have this heading: "A Psalm of David." Others are marked with such names as Moses, Solomon, Asaph, Heman, Ethan, and the sons of Korah.

But these psalm titles can be misleading. "A Psalm of David," for instance, might actually mean "A Psalm *About* David," "A Psalm *for* David," "A Psalm *Like* David's," or "A Psalm *by* David." No one knows when or by whom the titles of the psalms were added. No one knows exactly what all of the titles mean. They need not be considered a part of the inspired Word of God; instead, they are a very ancient attempt to write an explanation of the Psalms.

Bible scholars disagree about when the Psalms were written. Most agree that some of them may have appeared even before King David's time, but others long after. It is clear that more than one person was inspired by God to write Psalms.

To tell the truth, it is probably less important to know when

a psalm was written, or by whom, than it is to know these facts about any other part of the Bible. For the Psalms are for all people of all times. If you have ever read them very much, with a thinking mind and a feeling heart, you have no doubt found yourself saying: "Why . . . that's right! That's the way I feel sometimes. And that's how it is in my relationship with God."

All the main ideas found in Psalms have to do with God and man: realizing that God is near, giving thanks and praise to God, enjoying personal fellowship with God, remembering God's mighty acts, asking God's help in times of trouble.

These great ideas are expressed in an amazing variety of ways. The creation of the world, mighty cedars of Lebanon, sheep and shepherds, lions that prowl by night, frightened sailors in storms at sea, stately processions marching into the Temple—these and many other scenes are pictured in vivid, colorful words.

How about music for these great hymns? The original tunes have been lost in the mists of history. But God's people through the years—Jews and Christians—have never stopped singing the Psalms. To give only one example, *Baptist Hymnal* includes musical settings for ten psalms. Other hymnbooks have more.

There is no particular point in trying to outline the book of Psalms. In early times there seem to have been five small collections which were later combined: chapters 1-41; 42-72; 73-89; 90-106; 107-150. But there are many different types of songs within each of these five sections.

Everyone has his own list of favorite psalms. Most people would include at least this dozen: chapters 1; 8; 19; 23; 32; 46; 51; 100; 103; 104; 121; 122. Jesus quoted Psalm 22 as he was dying on the cross. There are a hundred other New Testament references to Psalms. What are *your* favorite psalms?

REVELATION

Revelation is the last book of the Bible. Thus it is also the last book of the New Testament—the only New Testament book classified as Prophecy.

Actually, "apocalypse" is a better word than "prophecy" to describe Revelation. In fact, the book begins with this word in its original Greek-language version.

The explanation of the book of Daniel in this section tells about some of the characteristics of apocalypse. All of these characteristics are found in Revelation, along with an amazing number of quotations from and references to the Old Testament.

The writer of Revelation calls himself "John" (Revelation 1:9) but never says which John. Many Bible scholars believe he was the apostle John; others think he was another early Christian with the same name. Exiled to the Mediterranean island of Patmos because of preaching the gospel, he had tremendous visions there which he recorded for all time to come.

The last book of the Bible is sometimes overworked and sometimes underworked. Christians through the ages have tried to understand its strange and startling events. Sometimes there seem to have been as many different explanations, however, as there were people doing the explaining!

Because of disagreements over meanings, and because some well-intentioned Christians have heatedly urged their own odd schemes based on Revelation, many other people have avoided the book entirely. This is a pity, for it contains much that every follower of Christ ought to read. Even with help he may not "get" all of it. But he will understand enough to make his reading worthwhile.

Probably you will appreciate a good commentary more when reading Revelation than when reading any other book of the Bible. And be sure to read Revelation in a modern translation.

All the lack of agreement about Revelation cannot hide its basic message, which holds true no matter how you interpret the book: There is great and powerful evil in the world. But the Lord Jesus Christ is greater than the forces of evil. He will win the battle, and those who put their trust in him can confidently face the future, in this world and the next.

ROMANS

Romans is a book of the New Testament—the first, longest, and most important book in the section called Paul's Letters.

Many of Paul's Letters grew out of emergencies—false teachers upsetting Christians somewhere, divisions among church membership, or something like that.

Romans is different. Paul had more time on his hands than usual while he was in Corinth, about A.D. 58. He had not yet visited Rome and knew of no particular problem among the small group of believers there. One reason he wrote them a letter was to help prepare the way for his hoped-for trip to Rome. And in this long letter, Paul made his fullest, clearest, best-organized statement of what he believed and taught—about God, about man, about the Lord Jesus Christ.

The key word of Romans is *righteousness*. By righteousness Paul did not mean what often comes to the minds of people today: a goody-goody sort of religion, looking for right deeds and shaming wrong ones. Instead, for Paul righteousness meant first of all that God himself is righteous; that is, he is trustworthy, loyal, faithful to his promises. He kept the covenant he made in olden times with Abraham and Abraham's descendants. He keeps his covenant now with all who entrust their lives to him. And righteousness for a human being means right relationship to God. By faith in God through Jesus Christ man is saved, not by good works.

No wonder the book of Romans has sparked renewal and reformation time and again through the centuries! Whenever Christians stray away from the basic truth that righteousness and salvation come from *God*, not man, Paul's letter calls them back.

Romans is not the easiest of Bible books to read, but all Christians should read it. This outline may help:
1. How righteousness comes—by faith in God, not by being good (chapters 1-5).
2. What new life in Christ means to a Christian (6-8).
3. Why many of God's Chosen People of olden times—the Jews—have not accepted God's promised Christ or Messiah (9-11).
4. What a Christian ought to do—in the church and in the world (12:1 to 15:13).
5. Personal notes from Paul (15:14 to 16:27).

RUTH

Ruth is the shortest of twelve Old Testament books in the section called History. It tells one of the most beautiful stories in all the Scriptures.

A foreign girl, worshiper of an idol-god, Ruth married into a Hebrew family that had moved to Moab because of famine. Left a young widow, Ruth insisted on going back to Bethlehem with her Hebrew mother-in-law, also now a widow. There Ruth's love and loyalty were rewarded as she eventually married Boaz, a rich relative of her first husband.

Many people miss one of the most significant parts of Ruth: the last few verses in the fourth of its four brief chapters. There we are told why this story—interesting but seemingly not too important—was included in the inspired Word of God. Ruth became the great-grandmother of King David—and, through David, became an ancestress of Jesus himself.

Be sure to read all of Ruth. No better example of a short story exists in any of the world's literature.

1 SAMUEL

First Samuel is an Old Testament book of History. It is located about one fourth of the way from the front of the Bible.

Formerly 1 Samuel and 2 Samuel were combined, thus making the longest book in the Bible except Psalms. When the first Bible translation was made, the Greek Old Testament, these two books were divided to avoid having such a long scroll.

The book of 1 Samuel may well be described as a "hinge of history." In it the period of the judges—strong tribal chieftains who ruled for brief periods of time—came to an end. The Israelites were impressed with the way other nations around them were led into battle by kings. They decided that they wanted a king.

First Samuel was probably not written by Samuel—at least, not chapters 25-31, which tell of events after his death. However, Samuel is the first of three main characters we meet in the book.

Perhaps you already know about Samuel's early life—especially that favorite story of how God called him one night while he was still a boy, helping the old priest Eli in the house of the Lord. Samuel became one of the most attractive and successful leaders of God's Chosen People in all their long history. He has been called "the last of the judges" and "the first of the prophets." Another nickname that fits him is "the king-maker," since he anointed the first two men to serve as kings in Israel.

Tall and powerful, Saul looked every inch a king. Yet, he proved an utter failure. God directed Samuel instead to anoint a shepherd-boy of Bethlehem who was to become his country's greatest monarch. But first David lived through many adventures—killing the giant Goliath, becoming a sort of Robin Hood to escape jealous King Saul, winning battle after battle.

This outline will guide your reading of one of the Bible's most lively and exciting books:
1. Samuel's period of leadership (chapters 1-7).
2. The early part of the reign of King Saul (9-15).
3. The rise of young David (16-27).
   (1) He becomes known as giant-killer, warrior, and musician (16-20).
   (2) He is forced to become an outlaw chief (21-27).
4. The sad end of Saul's career (28-31).

2 SAMUEL

Second Samuel is an Old Testament book of History. Originally, 1 Samuel and 2 Samuel were two parts of the same book.

The book of 2 Samuel is not about Samuel nor by him. A more accurate title for today's readers might be: "David the King." First Samuel tells the early part of David's life before he came to the throne. Second Samuel is entirely composed of stories from the times of David's reign. It includes some of the most exciting, best-written narratives to be found in the ancient history of Israel or any other nation. But more than that: This chronicle of a great king was inspired by the Lord God himself.

No more winsome character than David appears anywhere in the Bible. Jealous King Saul had repeatedly tried to kill him; yet, when Saul died in battle, David mourned over the fallen hero—and over Prince Jonathan, the late king's son and David's dearest friend. David invited Jonathan's only son, "the little lame prince," to live in his palace. Supremely brave and gifted as a leader of men, David won greater victories than any other Israelite had ever done.

Yet the book of 2 Samuel does not try to hide David's faults. This is one sign that God guided the writing of Israel's history: Royal records of any other people would have contained nothing but praise for the king. Furthermore, the greatest sin of David's life—arranging the death of a bold warrior and taking the dead man's wife—would have been considered usual behavior for most monarchs. But David was accused to his face by the prophet Nathan, and both he and his people suffered because of his wrongdoing.

Other striking characters crowd the pages of 2 Samuel: Absalom, long-haired rebel prince; Joab, stubborn and cruel commander-in-chief; Bathsheba, whose beauty led David astray; Barzillai, aged country squire who helped David when the king was temporarily a refugee from his own hard-won capital city.

Do you like adventure stories—of courage and heroism? Then read 2 Samuel—all of it. But remember as you read that not even noble King David knew the love taught and shown by Jesus Christ. Jesus was yet to be born as David's many-great's-grandson!

SONG OF SOLOMON

The Song of Solomon is a book of the Old Testament—the last and shortest of five books classified as Poetry.

Certainly "poetry" is a fitting term for this book. No more lovely lyrics exist in any language. Note this one (2:10-13, RSV):

> Arise, my love, my fair one,
>   and come away;
> for lo, the winter is past,
>   the rain is over and gone.
> The flowers appear on the earth,
>   the time of singing has come,
> and the voice of the turtledove
>   is heard in our land.
> The fig tree puts forth its figs,
>   and the vines are in blossom;
>   they give forth fragrance.
> Arise, my love, my fair one,
>   and come away.

It may seem strange that such simple love songs as these have been interpreted in all sorts of peculiar ways. The majority of Bible scholars today, however, agree that the Song of Solomon is just what it seems to be: a collection of romantic poems suitable for a wedding feast. At such celebrations in old Palestine, the groom was often honored as the greatest of kings. This may be why the book begins: "The Song of Songs, which is Solomon's." (King Solomon himself could have been the inspired writer.)

Some Christians, past and present, have made the mistake of thinking that anything having to do with sex is wrong and dirty. Other people, especially in today's world, make the opposite mistake of thinking that human bodies may be used as sex playthings.

Perhaps God caused the Song of Solomon to be placed in our Bible for such times as these. The poems are frank and free in their descriptions of physical charm and sexual attraction. But they also paint a clear picture of how God intended his good gift of sex to be used: in holy marriage that helps both husband and wife to find joy and fulfilment in loving, loyal union.

1 THESSALONIANS

First Thessalonians is a New Testament book, located in the section called Paul's Letters. Many Bible scholars believe it was the first letter Paul wrote among the thirteen that are in our Bible.

In Paul's day, Thessalonica was an important seaport city and naval base in northern Greece. (It is still that today; only the first four letters have been dropped from its ancient name.) On his second missionary journey the apostle Paul stopped there—perhaps for only three weeks, perhaps longer. Several people, both Greeks and Jews, believed Paul's preaching about the Lord Jesus Christ. However, his enemies stirred up trouble, and Paul had to leave town rather suddenly.

After leaving Thessalonica, Paul sent his young helper Timothy back to see how the new church there was getting along. Sometime in the year A.D. 50 or 51, while Paul was living at Corinth, Timothy came to make his report.

Things were going well in Thessalonica. In spite of Paul's being forced to leave them so soon, the new Christians there were growing as a congregation should. A few problems had appeared, but no serious ones.

In joy and gratitude Paul dashed off the letter we call 1 Thessalonians. Besides praising the believers in Thessalonica for their progress in the faith, he also tried to help them with problems they were facing. Two of these had to do with the second coming of the Lord Jesus. "If he is coming back soon," some Thessalonian Christians were asking, "then why should we work at our regular jobs? Why shouldn't we just spend all our time in prayer and good works?" Other church members were worried about Christian relatives and friends who had already died: "What will become of them when Christ returns?"

In writing about the second coming of our Lord, Paul did not do as some Christians have done. He did not put out all sorts of schemes and speculations about the future—exactly when that day will be, and so on. Instead, Paul's teachings about Christ's return were based on what Christ had already done, and on what Christ was now doing through the lives of believers.

In the meantime, Paul urged his Thessalonian friends to live right, work hard, and keep their faith in the Lord.

2 THESSALONIANS

Second Thessalonians is one of the shortest books in the section of the New Testament called Paul's Letters.

The message from the apostle Paul that we call 1 Thessalonians did not solve all the problems in that young church. In fact, it may have caused some of them to get worse. Paul's explanations about the return of Christ made some Thessalonian Christians even more eager to do nothing but wait for that blessed day. Their laziness was beginning to give Christians a bad name in the city.

There also seem to have been troublemakers who deliberately tried to work against Paul. Either 1 Thessalonians was said not to be a genuine letter from Paul, or else another letter had been sent with his name falsely attached.

Again Paul wrote to Thessalonica. In three brief chapters he stressed once more the main points he had made in the five chapters of 1 Thessalonians: Christ's future return and Christians' present responsibility to work hard—in faith, hope, and love.

1 TIMOTHY

First Timothy is grouped with other New Testament books called Paul's Letters. It, with the two letters just after it, also make up a special subgroup called the Pastoral Epistles. They were not written to all members of a church or churches, but to pastors of the churches—specifically, to Timothy and to Titus.

Many questions have been raised about the Pastoral Epistles. For at least four reasons many people wonder how those books relate to the rest of Paul's Letters:

1. They do not match any of Paul's life story as told in the book of Acts. For instance, 1 Timothy says that Paul once left Timothy in charge of the church at Ephesus. Acts does not.

2. They use many Greek words not found in Paul's other writings, and do not use words that are found elsewhere.

3. They seem to speak of times when churches had become more highly organized, with certain classes of leaders, such as bishops, deacons, and elders.

4. They stress right doctrines, church order, and opposition to false teachers more than they do the things Paul emphasized in his other letters: faith in Christ and leadership of the Holy Spirit.

No one has a perfect solution for these problems. Some people say that a Christian of later times must have put into writing what he had heard Paul teach and preach. Other people insist that only Paul himself could have written the Pastoral Epistles.

How thankful we should be, then, that the Bible depends on God, not man, for its authority! No matter who may have been inspired to write a Bible book, no matter what opinions people may have about it, we can find in it God's message for our own need and our own day.

Here are a few of the memorable passages in 1 Timothy:

1. Hymns and prayers used by the early church (1 Timothy 1:17; 3:16; 6:15-16).

2. Good fatherly advice to all young Christians, first addressed to Timothy (1 Timothy 4:12; 5:1-2; 6:11-12).

3. The saving grace of Jesus Christ, shown to and through the apostle Paul (1 Timothy 1:12-16; 2:3-7).

2 TIMOTHY

Second Timothy is a book of the New Testament, in the section called Paul's Letters. It, along with the book just before it and the book just after it in Bible order, is also called one of the Pastoral Epistles.

The previous section about 1 Timothy tells why many people have questioned whether the apostle Paul really did write 1 Timothy, 2 Timothy, and Titus. Notice again, though, that the truth of the Scriptures does not rest on the men who wrote them but on the God who inspired them.

Second Timothy was apparently written at a time when Paul was in prison in Rome. However, it hardly fits in with the Roman imprisonment told about in the last chapter of Acts. Paul seems to have been set free for a while, then jailed again.

Many Christians, even though knowing the serious problems raised about when, where, and by whom 2 Timothy was written, yet find it hard to believe that this book is not just what it seems to be: the last thing Paul ever wrote.

Notice especially the fourth and final chapter of 2 Timothy. In it Paul speaks as if he knew the end of his life was near (2 Timothy 4:6-8). He longed to see Timothy once more—his son in the faith (2 Timothy 4:9,21). Apparently cold in his dungeon cell, Paul asked Timothy to bring along a warm cloak (2 Timothy 4:13). Everyone had deserted Paul in prison—everyone except faithful Dr. Luke, who must have written down this letter at Paul's dictation (2 Timothy 4:10-11).

Like 1 Timothy, 2 Timothy also contains what may have been an early Christian hymn: 2 Timothy 2:11-13. It also includes one of the clearest statements anywhere in the Bible of the value of the Bible itself: 2 Timothy 3:14-17.

Second Timothy 2:1-8 is an especially good passage for a young Christian to read. Paul never promised anybody that it was easy to be a Christian. Instead, he drew examples from the life of a soldier, an athlete, and a farmer, to urge that Timothy must be strong and brave, no matter what might come. And in verse 8, he reminded Timothy of the most important thing of all: the good news about Jesus Christ.

TITUS

Titus is a book of the New Testament—the next to the last and next to the shortest in the section classified as Paul's Letters. It, along with 1 Timothy and 2 Timothy, also helps make up a special subgroup known as the Pastoral Epistles.

The preceding sections about the Timothy letters tell why many Christians wonder how the Pastoral Epistles fit in with Paul's other writings, and with the story of Paul's life as told in the book of Acts. For instance, according to the book of Titus, Paul and Titus must have worked together as missionaries on the Mediterranean island of Crete, and then Paul left Titus there to continue the job. Nothing at all like this is mentioned in Acts. It would seem that any such events must have happened between the end of Paul's first imprisonment (described in the last chapters of Acts) and a second imprisonment (mentioned but not clearly explained in the book of 2 Timothy).

The Bible tells us little about Titus. He was not a Jew, and Paul resisted efforts to force him to observe Jewish laws; notice Galatians 2:1-5. He served as Paul's helper and messenger—in Corinth and probably in other places as well.

The book of Titus stresses some of the same things emphasized in 1 and 2 Timothy: setting up leaders for churches, promoting true teaching and right behavior, fighting false doctrines and bad conduct.

Two important facts about Christianity, which sometimes seem to contradict each other, are clearly stated in the third of Titus' three brief chapters: Christians are saved by a new spiritual birth that comes from God's grace and mercy in Jesus Christ, not from good deeds than they themselves do (Titus 3:5-7). But those who have believed in Christ are then supposed to show their faith, and to bear fruit as Christians, by doing good works (Titus 3:8,14).

ZECHARIAH

Zechariah is the longest book in the last section of the Old Testament, the Minor Prophets.

Reading about two other prophetic books can help you understand more about the book of Zechariah: Daniel, because parts of Zechariah, like parts of Daniel, are in the form of an apocalypse; and Haggai, because the prophet Zechariah, like the prophet Haggai, encouraged the rebuilding of the Temple at Jerusalem.

Zechariah contains more prophecies than any other book of the Minor Prophets about the coming Messiah. Some of them may still wait to be fulfilled till the promised return of Christ. But others came true in the life and work of Jesus. One of the most famous of these is Zechariah 9:9, which pictures the Messiah-King riding on a simple donkey, a common beast of burden, not on a great prancing war-horse as other kings did. Do you remember what the Prince of Peace rode when he led a great procession into Jerusalem? (See Matthew 21:1-11.)

ZEPHANIAH

Zephaniah is one of twelve short Old Testament books grouped as Minor Prophets. It is fourth from last in order in the Old Testament, and the last Bible book in alphabetical listing.

The prophet Zephaniah was related to the royal family of Judah, the Southern Kingdom. He was born during the reign of wicked King Manasseh, who persecuted worshipers of the true God. Zephaniah's parents must have trusted the Lord's ability to shelter his faithful followers because they called their son by a name that means "God hides."

Later, during the reign of King Josiah, the prophet Zephaniah spoke out against wickedness and idol worship. He warned that the Lord God would bring terrific punishment on all nations—including the Chosen People of Judah.

The Scythians, a fierce tribe from what is now southern Russia, invaded Judah during the times of Zephaniah. Maybe the destruction caused by their wild raids helped Zephaniah to compose his inspired prophecies. Certainly no book of the Bible paints a more dreadful picture of an angry God than do these three brief chapters.

It is more pleasant—and much more important—that we read and study other parts of the Bible that stress God's love. But such books as Zephaniah help us remember that there is another side to the coin: Those who despise God's love can sooner or later expect to feel the pangs of God's wrath.

5
HOW TO USE BIBLE HELPS

Keith was comparing his Bible with his mother's. "Why is yours so much thicker than mine, Mom?" he asked.

Mother turned to the back of her Bible. "Look, Keith. See all these Bible helps? My Bible has a concordance, a dictionary, and several maps in it. No wonder it's thicker!"

Keith glanced back at the Bible in his hand. "I wish my Bible had some helps in it, too."

Actually, Keith's Bible does have Bible helps. All Bibles in use nowadays have helps in them. But the helps in Keith's Bible are not the same as those in the back of his mother's Bible.

What are the different kinds of Bible helps? Why is each type useful? How can they help you understand the Bible better?

Helps Found in All Bibles

Every Bible being printed these days, no matter how simple or inexpensive, has some Bible helps in it. That is, it has some information added to the actual words of the Bible to help you understand those words and read them more easily.

The most common types of Bible helps are *chapter and verse markings.* Had you ever stopped to think that the original Hebrew Old Testament and Greek New Testament were not divided into verses? Some parts of them were not even divided into chapters. Numbers for chapters and verses, and the places where these numbers are printed—all of this is the work of people who lived long after the Bible was written.

Can you see why chapter and verse markings are important Bible helps? Can you imagine how hard it would be to find Acts 16:31, for instance, if these were the only directions anyone could give you: "It's a little past the middle of the book, just after Paul arrived in Philippi, and before he traveled on to Thessalonica"?

Older Bible translations print each verse as if it were a separate paragraph. It is indented, with its number in front, like this:

31 And they said, Believe on the Lord Jesus Christ.

However, even in these older translations, you will find proof that not every verse is really a separate paragraph. Often you will see this sign after a verse number: ¶. This is a "new paragraph" sign. It means that some Bible publisher decided that a new subject or a new thought began with that particular verse.

This is why newer translations do not usually print verse numbers as large as older translations do. Many people who study the Bible have come to realize that chopping it up into short verses often makes it harder to read with full understanding.

Most newer Bible versions print paragraphs as in any other book of prose—and in poetic sections, print lines as in any other book of poetry. Verse numbers are made small and printed just above the first word of the verse, like this: [31] **And they said, "Believe in the Lord Jesus."** Sometimes verse (and chapter) numbers are even moved out to the margin of the page. You can tell where a new verse begins by spotting a punctuation mark that shows a break in thought.

Chapter and verse markings are useful Bible helps. It would take much longer to find things in the Bible if we didn't have them. But remember: They are not perfect, nor are they a part of the inspired Word of God. They are just Bible helps.

Titles are Bible helps of the same type as chapter and verse markings. Bible books as first written did not have titles. These were added later. In section 4 of this book, you will find interesting information about how some of the Bible books got their present titles.

Not every book title in every version of the Bible can be absolutely depended upon. For instance, many older Bibles print this title: "The Epistle of Paul the Apostle to the Hebrews." Actually, the book of Hebrews itself nowhere says that Paul wrote it. Most Bible scholars today agree that someone other than Paul was the inspired writer of Hebrews—who, no one knows. That's why most newer Bibles simply print the title as: "The Epistle to the Hebrews," or "A Letter to Jewish Christians."

The book of Psalms has titles for many individual chapters, besides a title for the whole book. Some people make the mistake of thinking that these titles are a part of the Bible itself. They say that chapters entitled "A Psalm of David," for instance, *prove* that David wrote these psalms.

The chapter titles in the book of Psalms are very old. No one knows who added them. But remember: They are additions, even though ancient ones. They are not a part of the original inspired Word of God. They are just Bible helps.

Helps Found in Some Bibles

Many Bibles, besides having chapter and verse markings and titles, also have *headlines.* Perhaps you've never thought of them as headlines, because they are not printed in such big letters as newspaper headlines. But they are headlines just the same.

Headlines most often appear at the tops of Bible pages. At a glance you can get a clue to what that page of the Bible is mainly about. Many Bibles also print headlines at the beginnings of chapters. Some Bibles, especially newer translations, print headlines at the beginnings of shorter sections within chapters. All of these are Bible helps—useful in reading the Bible, but not a part of the Bible itself.

Many Bibles also print different types of *notes.* Sometimes these are footnotes, appearing at the bottom of the page. Sometimes they are center-column notes, printed in a narrow list that runs down the middle of the page. Sometimes they are stuck into Bible verses themselves, or beside them or between them; usually such notes are printed in smaller letters, or in italics, or placed in parentheses, or marked somehow so that you can know they are just notes, not a part of the Bible itself.

Probably the most common type of notes can tell you where to find other verses that are alike in some way with the verse you are reading. Maybe an important word or idea is repeated in that other verse; maybe the same Bible character or place or

---

958   CHAPTER 1.

1 John Baptist's office. 9 Jesus baptized : 12 he is tempted, 14 preacheth, 16 calleth Peter and others, 32 and cureth many.

THE beginning of the gospel of Jē'ṣus Chrīst, ᵃ the Son of God ;

2 As it is written in the prophets, ᵇ Behold, I send my messenger before thy face, which shall prepare thy way before thee.

3 The ᶜ voice of one crying in the wilderness, Prepare ye the

A.D. 26.

ending.

CHAP. 1.

ᵃ Ps. 2. 7.
Luke 1. 35.
John 1. 34.
Rom. 8. 3.
1 John 4. 15.
ᵇ Mal. 3. 1.
ᶜ Isa. 40. 3.
Luke 3. 4.
John 1. 15, 23.
1 Or, unto.
ᵈ Lev. 11. 22.
ᵉ Acts 13. 25.

from Năz'ạ-rĕth o was baptized of Jͼ
10 And ' straigl up out of the wat heavens ᵃ opened, like a dove descenc
11 And there ͼ from heaven, *say* my beloved Son, well pleased.
12 And ᵏ immedi driveth him into t
13 And he was wilderness forty ͼ of Sā'tan ͼ and

event is featured in it. When you check the tiny number or letter of the alphabet or other code that leads your eye to such a verse reference, you can then look up that other verse and see how it helps you understand the verse you have just read. (Most Bibles explain somewhere, usually in the front or the back, what kind of code is used in notes.)

The type of notes just explained is sometimes called "cross reference" or "chain reference." But many Bibles have other kinds of notes as well. One of the most important of these other types can help you remember something which is explained in section 1 of this book.

The Bible was not first written in English, but rather in Hebrew, Aramaic, and Greek. It is hard to make English say exactly the same thing as those other languages say. Also, no original copies of Bible books still exist. The oldest copies available do not always read exactly the same, mainly because they were written by hand, and even the best writer will make mistakes sometimes.

Some Bible notes explain that a verse could be stated more than one way in good clear English. The best way of saying it, the one probably closest to what the original inspired writer meant, is printed in the verse itself. But another possible way of saying it may be printed in a note somewhere on the same page.

Other notes explain that not all ancient copies of the Bible agree on the wording of some verses. Different notes use different terms to describe these oldest Bibles still in existence. Sometimes they are called "manuscripts"; sometimes, "witnesses"; sometimes, "authorities." In Bible notes using any of these terms, you may find out just how and where these oldest copies disagree. (And, if you stop to think about it, you will be amazed to find out how often all the important copies *do* agree!)

Many other types of notes are printed in different kinds of Bibles. In fact, all of the Bible helps described in the last part of this section may also be found (in a short form) bound into the same volume with a Bible. But remember: All of them are Bible helps, not parts of the Bible itself.

Helps Usually Found in Separate Books

A *concordance* is a highly useful Bible help, especially when you have read the Bible enough that you can recall parts of favorite verses.

' Suppose, for instance, that you are thinking of "God is love." You would like to know how the rest of that verse reads, and where it is found in the Bible. That's when you need a concordance.

Start with an important word in the part of the verse that you can remember. "Love" would be a better word to look for than "God," because "God" is found in so many thousands of Bible verses.

A concordance is arranged by alphabet, like a dictionary. Look up "love." You should find something like this:

LOVE
1 John 4:8   He who does not *love* does not know God; for God is *love*.
1 John 4:16   God is *love,* and he who abides in *love* abides in God.

Now you can easily find these two verses in your Bible, and decide which of them it was you had in mind.

If you don't find the verse you're trying to remember, think of some other important word in it. To use the same example, if you don't find "God is love" under the word "love," then try the word "God."

A truly complete concordance is an immense book—thicker than almost any Bible. In such a concordance, you could even find "God is love" by looking up the word "is." Most concordances, however, only include the more important words and the

---

sincerely   602

sincerely
now if ye have done truly and *s.*
    Judg 9:16, 19*
one preach Christ, not *s. Phil 1:16*

sincerity
serve the Lord in *s.* and. *Josh 24:14*
unleavened bread of *s.*   *1 Cor 5:8*
in godly *s.* we have had. *2 Cor 1:12*
but as of *s.* in the sight of God. 2:17
to prove *s.* of your love.   8:8
them that love our Lord Jesus in *s.*
    Eph 6:24
doctrine shewing gravity, *s. Tit 2:7*

sinew
Israel eat not of the *s.* that shrank
. . . Jacob in the *s.*   *Gen 32:32*
thy neck is an iron *s.*   *Isa 48:4*

sinews

I will **sing**
I will s. to the Lord.   *Ex 15:1*
    Judg 5:3; Ps 13:6
my heart is fixed, *I will s. Ps 57:7*
I will s. unto thee among the.   9
I will s. of thy power, of. 59:16; 89:1
O my strength, *will I s.* for God. 17
I will s. of mercy and judgement.
    101:1
I will s. unto the Lord as.   104:33
I will s. a new song unto.   144:9
will I s. to my wellbeloved a song.
    Isa 5:1
for this cause *will I s. Rom 15:9*
I will s. with the spirit, and *I will s.*
    with understanding. *1 Cor 14:15*
see **praise, praises**

singed
nor an hair of their head *s. Dan 3:27*

singlen
with gladness and *s.*

servants, be obedien
    heart.   *Eph*

singul
shall make a *s.* vow.

sink
I *s.* in deep mire whe
out of the mire, and I
thus shall Babylon *s.*
so that they began to
let these sayings *s.* d

sinnec
Pharaoh *s.* yet more.
Ye have *s.* a great si
whosoever hath *s.* a
    will I blot out of m

more familiar verses. Some concordances are even small enough to be placed in the back of a Bible.

Often a concordance saves space by using abbreviations for names of Bible books. The key word under an entry may be shortened, too; for instance, under "LOVE," you may find "1 Jn 4:16 God is 1., . . . abides in 1. abides in God." Words are often skipped, to leave room just for the most important words—the ones a person is likeliest to recognize when he's trying to find a familiar phrase.

A *Bible dictionary* is another extremely useful Bible help. A regular dictionary may aid in Bible reading, just as in reading any other book. But a Bible dictionary includes words and phrases that are not found, or not as fully explained, in a regular dictionary.

Some Bible dictionaries are really encyclopedias, running to four or five volumes. For average Bible readers, however, one-volume Bible dictionaries are more useful. Sometimes a very brief Bible dictionary will be found in the back of a Bible.

Bible maps are valuable, too. A whole section or whole book of Bible maps is usually called a *Bible atlas*. These maps can be read like any other maps. The map legend will explain its markings. Often there will also be a list of Bible place-names, giving a number and a letter with each one so that you can track it down on the map.

A *Bible commentary* does just what its name sounds like: It makes comments about the Bible. These comments may be quite simple. Or, they may show the results of the most scholarly investigations.

Some Bible commentaries take up whole bookshelves. Others are only one volume long. In a sense, section 4 of this book may be considered a brief, basic Bible commentary. Other short commentaries are often bound in with Bibles themselves—either grouped at the front or the back, or divided and printed at the beginnings or endings of each Bible book.

A *harmony of the Gospels* is especially useful in reading Matthew, Mark, Luke, or John. If you have read more than one of these books about Jesus, then you know that many of the same events and teachings are repeated—some of them four times. A harmony of the Gospels uses parallel columns up and down the page to show which parts of these books match with one another.

It may have four columns for all four Gospels. Or, it may only have three columns for the three Gospels that are most alike: Matthew, Mark, and Luke.

A complete harmony prints all the verses themselves. It is actually the Gospels in one book, arranged in a different way from the usual order found in the New Testament. A shorter form of harmony only prints references to the verses, so that you can look them up in your own New Testament. Such a harmony is sometimes included with other helps at the back of a Bible.

The next section of this book, "Where to Find Interesting Parts of the Bible," is composed of two types of Bible helps that are slightly different from any of those described in this section. They have been included because you might not be as likely to find them elsewhere.

The main part of section 6 is called a "Bible Passage Finder." It lists alphabetically many words and phrases that might come to your mind when you try to recall a particular Bible story or a particularly interesting or important passage in the Bible. Along with that key word or phrase you will find a reference to the matching Bible verses.

The last part of section 6 suggests where to read in the Bible when you have certain thoughts or feelings, or when you find yourself in certain moods or situations. Remember: Reading the *Bible* is more important than reading any kind of *Bible helps!*

6
WHERE TO FIND INTERESTING PARTS OF THE BIBLE

Bible Passage Finder

ABEL AND CAIN (FIRST MURDER): Genesis 4.

ABRAHAM'S CALL: Genesis 12; 15.

ABSALOM'S HAIR: 2 Samuel 14:25-26; 18:1-33.

ADAM AND EVE (GARDEN OF EDEN): Genesis 2-3.

ADULTEROUS WOMAN: John 8:1-11.

AGONY OF JESUS (IN THE GARDEN): Matthew 26:30-56; Mark 14:26-50; Luke 22:39-54; John 18:1-12.

ANGELS' SONG: Luke 2:13-14.

ANNUNCIATION OF JESUS: Luke 1:26-38; Matthew 1:18-25.

APOSTLES, TWELVE: Matthew 10:1-4; Mark 3:13-19; Luke 6:12-16; Acts 1:13.

ARK, NOAH'S: Genesis 6-9.

ARK OF THE COVENANT: Exodus 25:10-22; 37:1-9.

ASCENSION OF JESUS: Luke 24:50-51; Acts 1:1-12.

BABEL, TOWER OF: Genesis 11:1-9.

BAPTISM OF JESUS: Matthew 3:13-17; Mark 1:9-11; Luke 3:21-22.

BARAK AND DEBORAH, SONG OF: Judges 4-5.

BATHSHEBA (AND DAVID'S GREAT SIN): 2 Samuel 11-12; Psalms 51; 32.

BEATITUDES: Matthew 5:1-12; Luke 6:20-23.

BEAUTIFUL GATE (PARALYZED MAN): Acts 3:1 to 4:22.

BETHESDA, POOL OF (PARALYZED MAN): John 5:1-18.

BIRTH OF JESUS: Matthew 1:18 to 2:12; Luke 2:1-20.

BIRTHRIGHT AND BLESSING (JACOB AND ESAU): Genesis 25:19-34; 27:1-45.

BORN BLIND: John 9.

BREAD OF LIFE: John 6:22-69.

BURNING BUSH (AND MOSES): Exodus 3:1-10.

CAIN AND ABEL (FIRST MURDER): Genesis 4.

CALL, MACEDONIAN: Acts 16:6-12.

CALL OF ABRAHAM: Genesis 12; 15.

CALL OF ISAIAH: Isaiah 6:1-8.

CALL OF MATTHEW: Matthew 9:9-13; Luke 5:27-32.

CALL OF MOSES (BURNING BUSH): Exodus 3:1-10.

CALL OF THE FISHERMEN: Matthew 4:17-22; Mark 1:14-20; Luke 5:1-11.

CALMING OF THE STORM: Matthew 8:23-27; Mark 4:35-41; Luke 8:22-25.

CALVARY: Matthew 27; Mark 15; Luke 23; John 19.

CARMEL, MOUNT (ELIJAH): 1 Kings 18.

CATCH OF FISH, MIRACULOUS: Luke 5:1-11; John 21:1-14.

CLEANSING OF THE TEMPLE: John 2:13-22; Matthew 21:12-17; Mark 11:15-19; Luke 19:45-48.
COMMANDMENTS, GREATEST: Matthew 22:34-40; Mark 12:28-34.
COMMANDMENTS, TEN: Exodus 20:1-17; Deuteronomy 5:6-21.
COMMISSION, GREAT: Matthew 28:16-20; Mark 16:15; Acts 1:8.
CONFESSION, GREAT (PETER'S): Matthew 16:13-20; Mark 8:27-30; Luke 9:18-21.
COUNCIL OF JERUSALEM: Acts 15:1-35; Galatians 2:1-10.
CREATION: Genesis 1-2; Psalms 104.
CROSSING OF THE JORDAN RIVER: Joshua 3-4.
CROSSING OF THE RED SEA: Exodus 14-15.
CROSS, THIEF ON THE: Luke 23:32-43.
CRUCIFIXION OF JESUS: Matthew 27; Mark 15; Luke 23; John 19.

DAMASCUS ROAD (SAUL OR PAUL): Acts 9:1-31; 22:5-21; 26:9-20.
DANIEL IN THE LIONS' DEN: Daniel 6.
DAVID'S GREAT SIN (AND BATHSHEBA): 2 Samuel 11-12; Psalms 51; 32.
DAVID AND THE GIANT GOLIATH: 1 Samuel 17.
DAY OF PENTECOST: Acts 2.
DEBORAH AND BARAK, SONG OF: Judges 4-5.
DECALOGUE: Exodus 20:1-17; Deuteronomy 5:6-21.
DELILAH AND SAMSON'S HAIR: Judges 16.
DELUGE: Genesis 6-9.
DEMONIAC, GADARENE OR GERASENE OR GERGESENE: Matthew 8:28-34; Mark 5:1-20; Luke 8:26-39.
DISCIPLES, TWELVE: Matthew 10:1-4; Mark 3:13-19; Luke 6:12-16; Acts 1:13.
DRY BONES: Ezekiel 37:1-14.

EDEN, GARDEN OF (ADAM AND EVE): Genesis 2-3.
ELIJAH AND THE WIDOW OF ZAREPHATH: 1 Kings 17.
ELIJAH ON MOUNT CARMEL: 1 Kings 18.
ELISHA AND THE SHUNAMMITE WOMAN: 2 Kings 4:8-37.
EMMANUEL: Isaiah 7:1-17; 8:5-8; Matthew 1:21-23.
EMMAUS, WALK TO: Luke 24:13-35.
ENDOR, WITCH OF: 1 Samuel 28.
ESAU AND JACOB (BIRTHRIGHT AND BLESSING): Genesis 25:19-34; 27:1-45.
ETHIOPIAN EUNUCH AND PHILIP: Acts 8:26-40.
EVE AND ADAM (GARDEN OF EDEN): Genesis 2-3.

FAITH CHAPTER: Hebrews 11.
FALL OF MAN (INTO SIN): Genesis 3.
FEEDING OF THE FIVE THOUSAND: Matthew 14:13-22; Mark 6:30-45; Luke 9:10-17; John 6:1-15.
FIERY FURNACE: Daniel 3.
FIRST CHRISTIAN MARTYR (STEPHEN): Acts 6-7.
FIRST MIRACLE OF JESUS: John 2:1-11.
FIRST MURDER (CAIN AND ABEL): Genesis 4.
FIRST PASSOVER: Exodus 12-13.
FIRST SIN: Genesis 3.
FISHERS OF MEN: Matthew 4:17-22; Mark 1:14-20; Luke 5:1-11.
FISH, MIRACULOUS CATCH OF: Luke 5:1-11; John 21:1-14.
FIVE LOAVES AND TWO FISHES: Matthew 14:13-22; Mark 6:30-45; Luke 9:10-17; John 6:1-15.

FLIGHT INTO EGYPT: Matthew 2:13-23.

FLOOD AND NOAH'S ARK: Genesis 6-9.

FOUR FRIENDS (PARALYZED MAN): Matthew 9:1-8; Mark 2:1-12; Luke 5:17-26.

FURNACE, FIERY: Daniel 3.

GADARENE DEMONIAC: Matthew 8:28-34; Mark 5:1-20; Luke 8:26-39.

GARDEN OF EDEN (ADAM AND EVE): Genesis 2-3.

GARDEN OF GETHSEMANE: Matthew 26:30-56; Mark 14:26-50; Luke 22:39-54; John 18:1-12.

GATE, BEAUTIFUL (PARALYZED MAN): Acts 3:1 to 4:22.

GERASENE (GERGESENE) DE-MONIAC: Matthew 8:28-34; Mark 5:1-20; Luke 8:26-39.

GIANT GOLIATH AND DAVID: 1 Samuel 17.

GIFT OF TONGUES: Acts 2:1-21; 10:44-48; 1 Corinthians 12-14.

GIFTS OF THE SPIRIT: 1 Corinthians 12-14.

GIRLS (VIRGINS), WISE AND FOOLISH: Matthew 25:1-13.

GLEANING IN THE FIELDS: Ruth 2.

GLORIA IN EXCELSIS DEO: Luke 2:13-14.

GOATS AND SHEEP: Matthew 25:31-46.

GOLDEN RULE: Matthew 7:12; Luke 6:31.

GOLGOTHA: Matthew 27; Mark 15; Luke 23; John 19.

GOLIATH THE GIANT AND DAVID: 1 Samuel 17.

GOMORRAH AND SODOM: Genesis 18:16 to 19:29.

GOOD SAMARITAN: Luke 10:25-37.

GOOD SHEPHERD: John 10:1-30.

GRAIN OF MUSTARD SEED: Matthew 13:31-32; 17:20; Mark 4:30-32; Luke 13:18-19; 17:5-6.

GREAT COMMISSION: Matthew 28:16-20; Mark 16:15; Acts 1:8.

GREAT CONFESSION (PETER'S): Matthew 16:13-20; Mark 8:27-30; Luke 9:18-21.

GREATEST COMMANDMENTS: Matthew 22:34-40; Mark 12:28-34.

GREAT FISH (WHALE) AND JONAH: Jonah 1-2.

HAIR, ABSALOM'S: 2 Samuel 14:25-26; 18:1-33.

HAIR, SAMSON'S (AND DELILAH): Judges 16.

HANDWRITING ON THE WALL: Daniel 5.

HEAVEN: Revelation 21-22.

HEAVEN, KINGDOM OF: Matthew 13.

HEBREW CHILDREN, THREE: Daniel 3.

HOLY, HOLY, HOLY: Isaiah 6:1-8; Revelation 4:1-11.

HOLY SPIRIT, OUTPOURING OF THE: Acts 2.

HOSANNA: Matthew 21:1-17; Mark 11:1-11; Luke 19:28-44.

HOUSE ON ROCK AND HOUSE ON SAND: Matthew 7:24-27; Luke 6:46-49.

IMMANUEL: Isaiah 7:1-17; 8:5-8; Matthew 1:21-23.

ISAAC, SACRIFICE OF: Genesis 22.

ISAIAH'S CALL (VISION): Isaiah 6:1-8.

ISSUE OF BLOOD: Matthew 9:20-22; Mark 5:24-34; Luke 8:42-48.

JACOB AND ESAU (BIRTHRIGHT AND BLESSING): Genesis 25:19-34; 27:1-45.

JACOB'S WELL: John 4:1-42.

JAILER, PHILIPPIAN: Acts 16:11-40.

JAIRUS' DAUGHTER, RAISING OF: Matthew 9:18-26; Mark 5:21-43; Luke 8:41-56.

JERICHO, WALLS OF: Joshua 6.

JERUSALEM COUNCIL: Acts 15:1-35; Galatians 2:1-20.

JERUSALEM, WALLS OF: Nehemiah 1-2; 4; 6.

JESUS' AGONY (IN THE GARDEN): Matthew 26:30-56; Mark 14:26-50; Luke 22:39-54; John 18:1-12.

JESUS' ASCENSION: Luke 24:50-51; Acts 1:1-12.

JESUS AT TWELVE YEARS OF AGE: Luke 2:40-52.

JESUS' BAPTISM: Matthew 3:13-17; Mark 1:9-11; Luke 3:21-22.

JESUS' BIRTH: Matthew 1:18 to 2:12; Luke 2:1-20.

JESUS' CLEANSING OF THE TEMPLE: John 2:13-22; Matthew 21:12-17; Mark 11:15-19; Luke 19:45-48.

JESUS' CRUCIFIXION: Matthew 27; Mark 15; Luke 23; John 19.

JESUS' DISCIPLES (TWELVE APOSTLES): Matthew 10:1-4; Mark 3:13-19; Luke 6:12-16; Acts 1:13.

JESUS' FIRST MIRACLE: John 2:1-11.

JESUS' PASSION (WEEK): Matthew 21-27; Mark 11-15; Luke 19-23; John 12-19.

JESUS' RESURRECTION: Matthew 28; Mark 16; Luke 24; John 20-21; Acts 1:1-9; 1 Corinthians 15.

JESUS' TEMPTATION: Matthew 4:1-11; Mark 1:12-13; Luke 4:1-13.

JESUS' TRANSFIGURATION: Matthew 17:1-13; Mark 9:2-13; Luke 9:28-36; 2 Peter 1:16-18.

JESUS' TRIUMPHAL ENTRY: Matthew 21:1-17; Mark 11:1-11; Luke 19:28-44.

JESUS' WALKING ON THE WATER: Matthew 14:22-33; Mark 6:45-51; John 6:15-21.

JONAH AND THE GREAT FISH (WHALE): Jonah 1-2.

JORDAN RIVER, CROSSING OF: Joshua 3-4.

JOURNEYS OF PAUL: Acts 13-28.

KINGDOM OF HEAVEN: Matthew 13.

LABORERS IN THE VINEYARD: Matthew 20:1-16.

LAST JUDGMENT: Matthew 25:31-46; Revelation 20:11-15.

LAST SUPPER: Matthew 26:17-30; Mark 14:12-26; Luke 22:7-27; John 13:1-30; 1 Corinthians 11:17-34.

LAZARUS AND THE RICH MAN: Luke 16:19-31.

LEGION (DEMONIAC): Matthew 8:28-34; Mark 5:1-20; Luke 8:26-39.

LIGHT OF THE WORLD: John 8:12; 9:1-5,39; Matthew 5:14-16.

LIONS' DEN (DANIEL): Daniel 6.

LITTLE GOSPEL: John 3:16.

LIVING WATER: John 4:7-14; 7:37-38; Jeremiah 2:11-13.

LORD'S PRAYER: Matthew 6:5-15; Luke 11:1-4.

LORD'S SUPPER: Matthew 26:17-30; Mark 14:12-26; Luke 22:7-27; John 13:1-30; 1 Corinthians 11:17-34.

LOST BOY: Luke 15:11-32.

LOST SHEEP: Luke 15:4-7; Matthew 18:12-14.

LOST SON: Luke 15:11-32.

LOVE CHAPTER: 1 Corinthians 13.

MACEDONIAN CALL: Acts 16:6-12.

MAGI: Matthew 2:1-12.

MAGNIFICAT: Luke 1:46-55.

MAN BORN BLIND: John 9.

MAN LET DOWN THROUGH THE ROOF: Matthew 9:1-8; Mark 2:1-12; Luke 5:17-26.

MAN WITH A WITHERED HAND: Matthew 12:9-14; Mark 3:1-6; Luke 6:6-11.

MARS' HILL (PAUL): Acts 17:15-34.

MARTYR, FIRST CHRISTIAN (STEPHEN): Acts 6-7.
MATTHEW, CALL OF: Matthew 9:9-13; Luke 5:27-32.
MIRACULOUS CATCH OF FISH: Luke 5:1-11; John 21:1-14.
MISSIONARY JOURNEYS OF PAUL: Acts 13-28.
MOSES AND THE BURNING BUSH: Exodus 3:1-10.
MOTHER-IN-LAW, PETER'S: Matthew 8:14-17; Mark 1:29-34; Luke 4:38-41.
MOUNT CARMEL (ELIJAH): 1 Kings 18.
MUSTARD SEED, GRAIN OF: Matthew 13:31-32; 17:20; Mark 4:30-32; Luke 13:18-19; 17:5-6.

NAAMAN THE LEPER: 2 Kings 5.
NABOTH'S VINEYARD: 1 Kings 21; 2 Kings 9:21-26.
NICODEMUS: John 3:1-21.
NOAH AND THE ARK (FLOOD): Genesis 6-9.

OUTPOURING OF THE HOLY SPIRIT: Acts 2.

PARABLE OF LAZARUS AND THE RICH MAN: Luke 16:19-31.
PARABLE OF THE GOOD SAMARITAN: Luke 10:25-37.
PARABLE OF THE LABORERS IN THE VINEYARD: Matthew 20:1-16.
PARABLE OF THE LOST BOY: Luke 15:11-32.
PARABLE OF THE LOST SHEEP: Luke 15:4-7; Matthew 18:12-14.
PARABLE OF THE LOST SON: Luke 15:11-32.
PARABLE OF THE PRODIGAL SON: Luke 15:11-32.
PARABLE OF THE PUBLICAN AND THE PHARISEE: Luke 18:9-14.
PARABLE OF THE RICH MAN AND LAZARUS: Luke 16:19-31.

PARABLE OF THE SOWER AND THE SEED: Matthew 13:1-23; Mark 4:1-20; Luke 8:4-15.
PARABLE OF THE TALENTS: Matthew 25:14-30.
PARABLE OF THE VINEYARD: Matthew 21:33-46; Mark 12:1-12; Luke 20:9-19.
PARABLE OF THE WHEAT AND THE TARES (WEEDS): Matthew 13:24-30,36-43.
PARABLE OF THE WISE AND FOOLISH VIRGINS (GIRLS): Matthew 25:1-13.
PARTING OF THE RED SEA: Exodus 14-15.
PASSION (WEEK) OF JESUS: Matthew 21-27; Mark 11-15; Luke 19-23; John 12-19.
PASSOVER (FIRST): Exodus 12-13.
PAUL ON MARS' HILL: Acts 17:15-34.
PAUL (SAUL) ON THE DAMASCUS ROAD: Acts 9:1-31; 22:5-21; 26:9-20.
PAUL'S MISSIONARY JOURNEYS: Acts 13-28.
PEARL OF GREAT PRICE: Matthew 13:45-46.
PENTECOST: Acts 2.
PETER'S GREAT CONFESSION: Matthew 16:13-20; Mark 8:27-30; Luke 9:18-21.
PETER'S MOTHER-IN-LAW: Matthew 8:14-17; Mark 1:29-34; Luke 4:38-41.
PETER'S VISION: Acts 10-11.
PHARISEE AND PUBLICAN: Luke 18:9-14.
PHILIP AND THE ETHIOPIAN EUNUCH: Acts 8:26-40.
PHILIPPIAN JAILER: Acts 16:11-40.
PLAGUES, TEN (IN EGYPT): Exodus 7-12.
POOL OF BETHESDA (PARALYZED MAN): John 5:1-18.
POTTER'S FIELD: Matthew 27:1-11.
POTTER'S WHEEL: Jeremiah 18:1-11.
PRODIGAL SON: Luke 15:11-32.

PUBLICAN AND PHARISEE: Luke 18:9-14.

QUEEN OF SHEBA: 1 Kings 10.

RAHAB AND THE TWO SPIES: Joshua 2:1-24; 6:22-25.
RAISING OF JAIRUS' DAUGHTER: Matthew 9:18-26; Mark 5:21-43; Luke 8:41-56.
RAISING OF LAZARUS: John 11:1-45.
RAISING OF THE WIDOW'S SON: Luke 7:11-17.
RED SEA, CROSSING (PARTING) OF THE: Exodus 14-15.
RESURRECTION OF JESUS: Matthew 28; Mark 16; Luke 24; John 20-21; Acts 1:1-9; 1 Corinthians 15.
RICH MAN AND LAZARUS: Luke 16:19-31.
RICH YOUNG RULER: Matthew 19:16-26; Mark 10:17-27; Luke 18:18-27.
ROAD TO DAMASCUS (SAUL OR PAUL): Acts 9:1-31; 22:5-21; 26:9-20.
ROOF, MAN LET DOWN THROUGH THE: Matthew 9:1-8; Mark 2:1-12; Luke 5:17-26.
ROOM ON THE ROOF: 2 Kings 4:8-37.
ROOM, UPPER: Mark 14:12-26; Luke 22:7-27; Acts 1:12-14.
RULER, RICH YOUNG: Matthew 19:16-26; Mark 10:17-27; Luke 18:18-27.

SACRIFICE OF ISAAC: Genesis 22.
SALT OF THE EARTH: Matthew 5:13.
SAMARITAN, GOOD: Luke 10:25-37.
SAMARITAN WOMAN AT THE WELL: John 4:1-42.
SAMSON'S HAIR (AND DELILAH): Judges 16.
SAUL (PAUL) ON THE DAMASCUS ROAD: Acts 9:1-31; 22:5-21; 26:9-20.

SEED AND THE SOWER: Matthew 13:1-23; Mark 4:1-20; Luke 8:4-15.
SERMON ON THE MOUNT: Matthew 5-7.
SERMON ON THE PLAIN: Luke 6:17-49.
SERVANT, SUFFERING: Isaiah 52:13 to 53:12.
SEVEN LAST WORDS: Luke 23:34,43; John 19:26-27; Matthew 27:46; Mark 15:34; John 19:28,30; Luke 23:46.
SEVENTY TIMES SEVEN: Matthew 18:15-35.
SHADRACH, MESHACH, ABED-NEGO (THREE HEBREW CHILDREN): Daniel 3.
SHEBA, QUEEN OF: 1 Kings 10.
SHEEP ·AND GOATS: Matthew 25:31-46.
SHEPHERD, GOOD: John 10:1-30.
SHEPHERD PSALM: Psalm 23.
SHEPHERDS (AND BABY JESUS): Luke 2:8-20.
SHIBBOLETH: Judges 12:1-6.
SHUNAMMITE WOMAN AND ELISHA: 2 Kings 4:8-37.
SIN, FIRST: Genesis 3.
SIN, UNFORGIVABLE: Matthew 12:22-32; Mark 3:20-30.
SLAUGHTER OF THE INNOCENTS: Matthew 2:16-18.
SOLOMON'S PORCH (PORTICO): John 10:22-39; Acts 3:1 to 4:4; 5:12-26.
SOLOMON'S TEMPLE: 1 Kings 5-8; 2 Chronicles 2-7.
SOWER AND THE SEED: Matthew 13:1-23; Mark 4:1-20; Luke 8:4-15.
SODOM AND GOMORRAH: Genesis 18:16 to 19:29.
SONG OF DEBORAH AND BARAK: Judges 4-5.
SPEAKING IN TONGUES: Acts 2:1-21; 10:44-48; 1 Corinthians 12-14.
SPIES, TWELVE: Numbers 13-14.
SPIES, TWO (AND RAHAB): Joshua 2:1-24; 6:22-25.

SPIRITUAL GIFTS: 1 Corinthians 12-14.
STEPHEN (FIRST CHRISTIAN MARTYR): Acts 6-7.
STILLING OF THE STORM: Matthew 8:23-27; Mark 4:35-41; Luke 8:22-25.
STONING OF STEPHEN: Acts 6-7.
SUFFERING SERVANT: Isaiah 52:13 to 53:12.
SYROPHOENICIAN WOMAN: Matthew 15:21-28; Mark 7:24-30.

TABERNACLE: Exodus 26-27; 31; 35-40.
TALENTS: Matthew 25:14-30.
TARES (WEEDS) AND WHEAT: Matthew 13:24-30,36-43.
TEMPLE (SOLOMON'S): 1 Kings 5-8; 2 Chronicles 2-7.
TEMPTATION OF JESUS: Matthew 4:1-11; Mark 1:12-13; Luke 4:1-13.
TEN COMMANDMENTS: Exodus 20:1-17; Deuteronomy 5:6-21.
TEN PLAGUES (IN EGYPT): Exodus 7-12.
THIEF ON THE CROSS: Luke 23:32-43.
THREE HEBREW CHILDREN (SHADRACH, MESHACH, ABED-NEGO): Daniel 3.
TONGUES, SPEAKING IN: Acts 2:1-21; 10:44-48; 1 Corinthians 12-14.
TOWER OF BABEL: Genesis 11:1-9.
TRANSFIGURATION OF JESUS: Matthew 17:1-13; Mark 9:2-13; Luke 9:28-36; 2 Peter 1:16-18.
TREE (ABSALOM'S HAIR): 2 Samuel 14:25-26; 18:1-33.
TREE (ZACCHAEUS): Luke 19:1-10.
TRIBES, TWELVE (OF ISRAEL): Genesis 49; Numbers 10:11-28; Deuteronomy 33; Revelation 7:1-7.
TRIUMPHAL ENTRY OF JESUS: Matthew 21:1-17; Mark 11:1-11; Luke 19:28-44.
TWELVE APOSTLES (JESUS' DISCIPLES): Matthew 10:1-4; Mark 3:13-19; Luke 6:12-16; Acts 1:13.
TWELVE SPIES: Numbers 13-14.
TWELVE TRIBES OF ISRAEL: Genesis 49; Numbers 10:11-28; Deuteronomy 33; Revelation 7:1-7.
TWELVE-YEAR-OLD JESUS: Luke 2:40-52.
TWO FISHES AND FIVE LOAVES: Matthew 14:13-22; Mark 6:30-45; Luke 9:10-17; John 6:1-15.

UNFORGIVABLE SIN: Matthew 12:22-32; Mark 3:20-30.
UPPER ROOM: Mark 14:12-26; Luke 22:7-27; Acts 1:12-14.

VINEYARD: Matthew 21:33-46; Mark 12:1-12; Luke 20:9-19.
VINEYARD, NABOTH'S: 1 Kings 21; 2 Kings 9:21-26.
VIRGIN BIRTH: Matthew 1:18-25; Luke 1:26-38; 2:1-7.
VIRGINS (GIRLS), WISE AND FOOLISH: Matthew 25:1-13.
VISION, ISAIAH'S: Isaiah 6:1-8.
VISION, PETER'S: Acts 10-11.

WALKING ON THE WATER: Matthew 14:22-33; Mark 6:45-51; John 6:15-21.
WALK TO EMMAUS: Luke 24:13-35.
WALL, HANDWRITING ON THE: Daniel 5.
WALLS OF JERICHO: Joshua 6.
WALLS OF JERUSALEM: Nehemiah 1-2; 4; 6.
WATER, LIVING: John 4:7-14; 7:37-38; Jeremiah 2:11-13.
WATER TURNED TO WINE: John 2:1-11.
WATER, WALKING ON THE: Matthew 14:22-33; Mark 6:45-51; John 6:15-21.
WEDDING AT CANA: John 2:1-11.
WEDDING FEAST: Matthew 22:1-14; 25:1-13; Luke 14:16-24.

WHALE (GREAT FISH) AND JONAH: Jonah 1-2.

WHEAT AND TARES (WEEDS): Matthew 13:24-30, 36-43.

WIDOW OF ZAREPHATH AND ELIJAH: 1 Kings 17.

WIDOW'S SON, RAISING OF THE: Luke 7:11-17.

WISE AND FOOLISH VIRGINS (GIRLS): Matthew 25:1-13.

WISE MEN: Matthew 2:1-12.

WITHERED HAND: Matthew 12:9-14; Mark 3:1-6; Luke 6:6-11.

WOMAN AT THE WELL: John 4:1-42.

WOMAN TAKEN IN ADULTERY: John 8:1-11.

WRITING ON THE WALL: Daniel 5.

ZACCHAEUS IN THE TREE: Luke 19:1-10.

ZAREPHATH, WIDOW OF (AND ELIJAH): 1 Kings 17.

Bible Reading Suggestions

IF YOU ARE . . .

. . . tempted to do wrong, read Psalms 15; 19; 139; Matthew 4:1-11; James 1.

. . . jealous of someone, read Psalms 49; 73.

. . . facing a hard decision, read Job 28:12-28; Isaiah 55.

. . . worried about something, read Psalm 46; Matthew 6:25-34.

. . . very tired, read Isaiah 40; Matthew 11:1-6,25-30.

. . . in need of forgiveness, read Psalm 86; Luke 15:11-32.

. . . made fun of for doing what is right, read Matthew 5:10-12; 1 Peter 4:12-19.

. . . leaving home, read Psalm 121; Proverbs 3:1-12.

. . . starting a new home, read Psalm 127; Ephesians 5:15 to 6:4; 1 Peter 3:1-9.

. . . starting a new job, read Psalm 1; Proverbs 16; Philippians 3:7-21.

IF YOU FEEL . . .

. . . discouraged, read Psalms 23; 42; 43.

. . . bored, read Job 38-39; Psalm 104.

. . . impatient, read Psalms 40; 90; Hebrews 12:1-14.

. . . lonely, read Psalms 27; 91.

. . . that friends have failed you, read Matthew 5:3-16,39-48; 1 Corinthians 13.

. . . that things are going from bad to worse, read 2 Timothy 3:1 to 4:18; Hebrews 13:1-21.

. . . that everything is going well, read Psalms 33; 100.

. . . that God seems far away, read Psalms 25; 125; 138.

. . . worried about those you love most, read Psalms 107; 111; 112.

. . . afraid of death, read 2 Corinthians 4:16 to 5:15; Revelation 7:9-17.

IF YOU HAVE. . .

. . . quarrelled with someone, read Matthew 18; James 3-4.

. . . done wrong, read Psalm 51; 1 John 1:5 to 2:6.

. . . been given a place of responsibility, read Joshua 1:1-9; Proverbs 2.

. . . a grudge against someone, read Luke 6:27-38; Romans 12; Ephesians 4:17-32.

. . . a hard job to do, read Ephesians 6:10-18; 2 Timothy 2:1-13.

. . . hard times in your life, read Colossians 1; 1 Peter 1; 4.

. . . sorrow because someone you love has died, read 1 Corinthians 15; 1 Thessalonians 4:13 to 5:11.

. . . trouble going to sleep, read Psalms 4; 56; 130.

. . . sickness or pain, read Psalms 6; 41; 103; Isaiah 26:3-4,7-12; James 5:13-18.

. . . too much to do, read Psalms 27; 91; Ecclesiastes 3:1-15; 12:1,13-14.

IF YOU WANT. . .

. . . a stronger faith in God, read Psalm 146; Hebrews 11:1 to 12:2.

. . . a mood of worship, read Psalms 96; 116.

. . . an inner peace, read John 14; Romans 8.

. . . to enjoy life, read Romans 6; Galatians 5:13-26.

. . . to make more money than you're making, read Psalm 37; Ecclesiastes 5:10-20.

. . . to get along well with other people, read Psalm 34; Romans 12.

. . . to do something special to help someone, read Matthew 6:1-4; James 2:1-9.

. . . to know how to use your money, read Matthew 6:19-24; Luke 16:1-15,19-31; 19:1-26.

. . . to know what heaven will be like, read John 14:1-6; 1 John 3:1-2; Revelation 21-22.

. . . to know how to be saved, read John 3:1-21; Acts 16:25-34; Romans 10:6-13.

7

HOW THE BIBLE CAME TO US

Long before there was a Bible, people who worshiped the Lord God loved to tell about him. As they sat around desert campfires under starry skies, they would sing of God's greatness and mercy. Grandfathers would pass on stories of how God had blessed and cared for them—and for their ancestors before them.

No one knows who first began to write down words that later became a part of the Bible. Many people think Moses was the first person inspired by God to do so. Certainly the books of Exodus and Deuteronomy speak of Moses writing laws, history, and songs.

Many other persons were led by God's Spirit to write down what they had learned about God and his dealings with men. Among important Bible characters besides Moses who are named as writers of parts of the Old Testament are David, Solomon, Isaiah, and Jeremiah. But there are others not so well known: Lemuel, for instance, and Agur, and Asaph, and Heman, and Ethan.

Many parts of the Old Testament do not mention an author's name at all. The book of Jonah, for instance, tells about the prophet Jonah; but it nowhere says that Jonah himself wrote the book. No one can tell how many different people God inspired to write parts of the Old Testament. The important fact is, God's Word got written. And God chose to use human beings—many different human beings—to get the job done.

The Story of Jesus Christ

Bible scholars think that the books of the Old Testament were gradually written over a period of nearly a thousand years. Throughout those centuries, God's Chosen People waited and hoped for the coming of a Savior, the Messiah or Christ. That hope was fulfilled in the life, death, and resurrection of Jesus of Nazareth.

Such an important event had to be told about. One of the first people to tell about it was the apostle Paul. He did not directly relate Jesus' life story; but through letters he wrote to Christians all over the Mediterranean world, he explained much about who Jesus is and how Jesus' followers ought to believe and behave.

Matthew, Mark, Luke, and John were four men inspired by God to write biographies of Jesus Christ. Luke also added another volume of biography and history, telling about the first generation who lived after the Lord Jesus went back to his heavenly glory with God. Other people—Peter and Jude and James and at least one early Christian whose name no one knows—wrote letters and teachings about the Christian faith and life.

Thus the twenty-seven books of the New Testament were written within a much shorter time-span than the thirty-nine books of the Old Testament. God had already guided Jewish Bible scholars to choose which of many religious books available to them were the right ones to be considered as God's Word. Now

Christians also met, discussed, exchanged letters, and followed God's guidance in deciding which of many Christian writings were also truly a part of God's Book of books, the Bible.

By the third century A.D., more than a thousand years after the earliest parts of it were put into writing, the Bible was complete. If you have already read section 1 of this book, you know that it was not written in languages most people nowadays can read. But its actual contents were exactly the same as what you will find in your own Bible today.

Into Languages of the People

Even when the complete Bible was still new, there were people who could not read it. In fact, even before there was a New Testament, Jewish scholars in Egypt had already translated the Old Testament from Hebrew into Greek. This was the Bible that Jesus himself knew.

During the times of Christ and after, the Roman Empire ruled much of the world. Romans used the Latin language. It isn't surprising, then, that the first translations of the New Testament were from Greek into Latin.

An important, complete translation of the Bible into Latin was made about four hundred years after Christ's birth by a devoted scholar named Jerome. Jerome's translation was nick-named the *Vulgate,* because *vulgar* or ordinary people could read and understand it. For many centuries the Vulgate was the main Bible used in Europe.

Other Bible translations were made in early days, too: into the languages of Egypt and Ethiopia and Armenia and Arabia. And through the centuries since then, as the story of Jesus has been told in more and more places, more and more new translations have been needed. At last count, there was at least one book of the Bible in each of 1,431 of the world's languages!

Since English is the language of this book and of its readers, let's pay special attention to how God's Word got into the English words that we can read today.

One of the main ancestor-languages of English was Anglo-Saxon. Parts of the Bible, including all four Gospels, were put into Anglo-Saxon by about A.D. 700. Here's how the Lord's Prayer looks in an Anglo-Saxon dialect of those times:

Fader uren thu in Heofnas, Sie gehalgud Nama thin; To Cymeth ric thin; Sie fillo thin Suae is in Heofne and in Eortha. Hlaf userne oferwirtlic sel us to daeg; and forgev us scyltha urna, suae we forgefon scylgum urum. And ne inlead writh in Cosnunge. Al gefrigurich from evil.

The first man to produce a complete Bible in English was named John Wycliffe. In the 1300's he became concerned because people could not read God's Word for themselves. So he not only translated the Bible; he also sent out his followers to teach it.

Here's how John Wycliffe translated the Lord's Prayer in 1382:

Oure fadir that art in heuenes, halwid be thi name; thi kyngdom cumme to, be thi wille don as in heuen so in erthe. Giv to vs this day oure breed ouer other substaunce; and forgeue to vs oure dettis, as we forgeue to oure dettours; and leede vs nat in to temptacioun, but delyuere vs fro yuel.

During the long years when most Bibles were in Latin only, religious leaders had gotten a strange idea. They thought that Bible-reading ought to be their own special monopoly. Thus many of them fought against such men as John Wycliffe, who insisted that everyone should read God's Word.

The invention of printing with movable type brought great changes to the world. The first complete book that Johann Gutenberg printed was the Bible—but it was still in Latin. With books becoming cheaper and more abundant, new ideas spread quickly. When Martin Luther and other European Christians decided it was time to reform Christianity by going back to the Bible, the news soon reached England.

William Tyndale was one of those most impressed by this news. Like Luther and other leaders of the Reformation, he saw how important it was to have the Word of God in clear, everyday language. A good Bible scholar, he set to work to make a new translation. Unlike John Wycliffe a century and a half before, Tyndale was able to go all the way back to the original languages of the Bible to make sure his translation was right.

In 1525 appeared the first printed New Testament in English. Because of opposition from religious leaders, copies of it had to be smuggled into England from Germany, where the printing had

been done. Here's how the Lord's Prayer reads in William Tyndale's translation:

**O oure father, which art in heven halewed be thy name. Let thy
kyngdom come. Thy wyll be fulfilled, as well in erth, as hit ys in heven.
Geve vs this daye oure dayly breade. And forgeve vs oure treaspases,
even as we forgeve them whych treaspas vs. Lede vs nott in to temptacion,
but delyvre vs from yvell.**

William Tyndale died for his faith before he could finish
translating the Old Testament as well. But his enemies were not
able to destroy all the copies of his work. Probably Tyndale had
more to do than any other one man with the English Bible as
it has been known throughout the centuries since he lived.

Even while Tyndale was in prison awaiting sentence of death,
other people were carrying on his work. Miles Coverdale published
in 1535 the first complete English Bible in print. Throughout the
1500's many other English versions of the Bible appeared—some

done by Protestants, some by Catholics; some by individuals, some by committees; some in England itself, some in other countries. (The Bible that the Pilgrims brought to New England in 1620 was called the Geneva Bible, after the Swiss city where it was published. This was also the first English Bible to divide chapters into verses.)

Authorized Versions

As early as 1539, a king of England had given his official approval to one particular version of the Bible. This one was called the Great Bible because of its huge size. A copy of it was placed in every church in England—chained to a desk, so people could read it but not take it home with them.

By the time of King James I, there were so many different Bibles in English that readers were confused. So the king called for a large committee of Bible scholars to compare all these earlier translations, check them against the original Greek and Hebrew, and produce a new version for his official approval. Thus there came into being the King James Version, in the year 1611.

Here's how the Lord's Prayer appears in the King James Version:

Our father which art in heauen, hallowed be thy name. Thy kingdome come, Thy will be done, in earth, as it is in heuen. Giue vs this day our daily bread. And forgiue vs our debts, as we forgiue our debters. And lead vs not into temptation, but deliuer vs from euil.

In the next 150 years after 1611, the King James Version was revised five times. Not till 1769 did the spelling in it become like that in Bibles still being printed today. During these same years, the King James Version (KJV) became the most popular of all Bibles in English. In fact, by the 1800's, many people thought of it as *the* Bible and didn't know there had ever been any other.

In many ways the King James Version deserves its high reputation. Its magnificent words ring throughout all English literature for three hundred years and find echoes in our everyday expressions even now. But it is not the best translation for people to read today for two basic reasons:

1. When the King James Version was being prepared, many of the oldest and most accurate copies of the Bible in its original languages had not yet been discovered. One of the oldest Greek

New Testaments was found in 1624, just thirteen years too late to help the KJV translators. Some of the oldest Hebrew manuscripts of Old Testament books were found in a cave near the Dead Sea by an Arab shepherd boy, as recently as 1947.

2. The English language has changed so much in more than three and a half centuries since 1611, that many verses in the King James Version simply make no sense at all to modern readers.

For these reasons, in the late 1800's Bible scholars began once more to revise the beloved old translation. Their work was published in 1881-85.

American Bible experts did not agree with some of the words used in this Bible. In 1901, by agreement with their English co-workers, they published their own American Standard Version.

But new manuscripts kept on turning up; and the English language kept on changing. Both Britons and Americans came to feel that those earlier revisions of the King James Version had not gone far enough in using clear, modern language. So, new committees of Bible scholars set to work again. The result is the Revised Standard Version. The New Testament was first published in 1946; the Old Testament, in 1952.

Here's how the Revised Standard Version (RSV) prints the Lord's Prayer:

"Our Father who art in heaven,
Hallowed by thy name.
Thy kingdom come,
Thy will be done,
    On earth as it is in heaven.
Give us this day our daily bread;
And forgive us our debts,
    As we also have forgiven our debtors;
And lead us not into temptation,
    But deliver us from evil."

Thus the RSV, used by millions of people throughout the world today, is a direct descendant of the King James Version of 1611, and of other authorized or official translations that came before and after it.

Many Translations

There have also been many "unauthorized" or "unofficial" translations of the Bible. The Hebrew Old Testament and Greek New Testament, of course, were written and even printed long before there were any copyright laws. So anyone has the right to prepare and publish his own wording of a Bible translation in any language.

Among the many men and women who have translated the New Testament or the complete Bible into English are John Wesley, founder of the Methodists, and Noah Webster, founder of the famous line of dictionaries. The best translation thus far prepared by a woman is the *Centenary Translation of the New Testament* by Helen Barrett Montgomery, first published in 1924.

Many translations—into English and other languages—have been sponsored or helped by Bible societies. Beginning in 1804 with the British and Foreign Bible Society, these organizations have been set up in many countries. Their goal is to get more copies of God's Word to more people, and to get more people to read it. In order to do this, they must often make new translations, or encourage others to do so.

One of the most interesting stories about newer translations comes from the worldwide work of the American Bible Society. Often it is hard or even impossible to find Christians who are familiar with both the language used in a certain country and with the original languages of the Bible. To help such people, the American Bible Society appointed Bible scholar Robert G. Bratcher to prepare a simple English translation.

The idea was to produce a Bible so understandable, so free of peculiar expressions, that someone who knew no Hebrew or Greek could still take it alone and from it hope to make a good, correct translation into any other tongue. Other intended users of this new translation were people who are learning English as a second language.

In 1966 *The New Testament in Today's English Version* was published, Because the expected number of readers was not too large, only one hundred thousand books were printed. What a surprise it was to the American Bible Society when millions of copies had to be printed even within the first year of publication!

At latest word, no less than 36 million copies of this New Testament translation had been sent out to people around the world. *The Old Testament in Today's English Version,* prepared by a committee headed by Bratcher, is expected to be ready by 1975.

Probably there are several reasons why TEV, as it has been nicknamed, is so popular. Bratcher's translation is one of the best and clearest ever published. Annie Vallotton's simple, modern line drawings add a special charm. The catchy title *Good News for Modern Man* attracts many readers. But above all, TEV's popularity shows that the Bible is still the most important and appealing Book in the world today–as it has been for ages past.

Here's how the Lord's Prayer comes out in *Today's English Version:*
"Our Father in heaven:
May your name be kept holy,
May your kingdom come,
May your will be done on earth as it is in heaven.
Give us today the food we need;
Forgive us the wrongs that we have done,

As we forgive the wrongs that others have done us;

Do not bring us to hard testing, but keep us safe from the Evil One."

Several Suggested Translations

This last section of BIBLE GUIDEBOOK has been extremely brief. There are at least two entire books that have the same title as this section: *How the Bible Came to Us.* Some of the most thrilling stories in all human history come from the writing, translating, publishing, and distributing of God's Word all over the world. There is no room to retell these exciting stories in these few pages.

But remember what this book has stressed several times: Reading the Bible is more important than reading books about the Bible. Therefore, this book comes to an end with a list of recent Bible translations suggested for your reading.

These are not all the English translations now in print. They are not even all the good English translations in print. They are

merely several of the best and most popular among many versions that have appeared in the twentieth century.

Good translations have been made of individual books of the Bible, or of groups of books (such as the Gospels or Paul's Letters). But all the versions listed here include the entire Bible, or at least the entire New Testament.

ASV—*American Standard Version*, 1901. This translation is described earlier in this section. A special revised edition of the ASV has been published in more recent years.

Weymouth—*The New Testament in Modern Speech* by Richard F. Weymouth, 1903. This was one of the earliest everyday language versions to become popular in modern times.

Moffatt—*The Bible, a New Translation* by James Moffatt, 1926. (The New Testament and Old Testament in this version had already appeared in 1913 and 1924.) Moffatt's work influenced other translations, also; he was a leading member of the committee that prepared the RSV.

Smith-Goodspeed—*The Complete Bible, an American Translation* by J. M. Powis Smith, Edgar J. Goodspeed, and others, 1931. (The two Testaments in this version had been published in 1923 and 1927.) The Smith-Goodspeed translation, as its title states, "speaks American." It uses clear, modern American English throughout.

Williams—*The New Testament, a Translation in the Language of the People* by Charles B. Williams, 1937. This modern-language Testament, like Phillips', has been consistently popular for some years.

Basic—*The Bible in Basic English* by S. H. Hooke and others, 1949. This unusual translation uses a total of only one thousand different English words.

Confraternity—*The Confraternity Edition of the Bible*, 1941-52. This important modern translation was prepared by a group of Roman Catholic Bible scholars.

RSV—*Revised Standard Version*, 1946-52. This translation is described earlier in this section.

Phillips—*The New Testament in Modern English* by J. B. Phillips, 1958. (Parts of the New Testament in Phillips' translation were published as early as 1947.) Phillips' work on the Old Testament is not yet complete.

Berkeley—*The Holy Bible: The Berkeley Version in Modern English* by Gerrit Verkuyl and others, 1945-1959. The Bible scholars who worked to produce this translation are generally considered conservative in their views on doctrine and biblical interpretation.

Amplified—*The Amplified Bible* by Frances E. Siewert and others, 1965. (The two Testaments in this version had been published earlier, in 1958 and 1962-64.) This translation almost becomes a Bible commentary, with various additions that are intended to make meanings clearer.

NEB—*The New English Bible* by Charles H. Dodd and others, 1961-70. In this entirely new translation, a group of British Bible scholars tried to get away completely from the influence of older versions and produce a Bible that would be as meaningful in this generation as the King James Version was in 1611. The result is a readable translation in the highest literary style.

TEV—The New Testament in *Today's English Version* was published by the American Bible Society in 1966. It is often identified by an alternate title, *Good News for Modern Man*. The Old Testament is to be published in 1976. This translation is marked by its simple, everyday language.

Jerusalem—*The Jerusalem Bible*, by Alexander Jones and others, 1966. This translation was prepared by a group of Roman Catholic Bible scholars. It uses the language we use today and has notes which explain many of the verses.

Living—*The Living Bible, Paraphrased* by Kenneth N. Taylor, 1971. Taylor's modern paraphrases (rewordings) of various groups of Bible books had been popular for several years before he completed paraphrasing the whole Bible.